# WHEN ALL YOU HAVE IS A HAMMER...

# AN INFORMATIONAL GUIDE TO SELF-DIRECTED IRAs

TERRY L. WHITE

President & CEO of Sunwest Trust, Inc.

ISBN 9781530136544

*Foreword*

"If all you have is a hammer, everything looks like a nail."
Bernard Baruch, American Businessman

When I was younger, during the summers I worked as a framer for my Dad's construction company. I used a big, heavy framing ax to pound 16-penny nails into 2 x 4s. I noticed that the finish carpenters on the site used a delicate, little hammer for their work of installing woodwork, windowsills, and molding. The tool I used for my work was not the right tool for the job of a finish carpenter, nor did I have the skill to become a finish carpenter; I recognized that.

You may wonder about the title of this book. With the foregoing story in mind, I chose the title for this book to position the Self-Directed IRA as another tool you may use to achieve your retirement goals. It is my opinion that Self-Directed IRAs are not for everyone; but for the right person, a Self-Directed IRA may be just the right tool for the job.

Self-Directed IRAs are great tools if you have the knowledge and skills about that in which you are investing; or want to acquire the knowledge and skills about that in which you want to invest; or are able to hire someone with the knowledge and skills about that in which you want to invest.

I wrote this book as an informational guide for those who may be interested in Self-Directed IRAs. It is my intention to give a broad overview of what owners of Self-Directed IRAs may expect and some of the investments they may purchase.

I hope this book is helpful to you.

Terry L. White

President & CEO Sunwest Trust, Inc.

# TABLE OF CONTENTS

# CHAPTER 1

## WHAT IS AN IRA?

An "IRA" is the acronym used for an Individual Retirement Arrangement. Individual Retirement Arrangements were introduced in 1974 through the Employee Retirement Income Security Act (ERISA) to provide a means for individuals to set aside money for retirement and also to provide certain tax advantages as an incentive for them to do so.

At the time of its introduction, most individuals relied on employer-sponsored retirement plans to save for retirement. If the employer did not offer a retirement plan, the individual did not have recourse to any other tax-advantaged retirement plan for savings. Further, when an employee left the employer, the employee had no place to move the retirement funds accumulated to date, making it necessary to leave the accumulated funds in the employer's retirement plan until reaching retirement age.

Subsequent amendments to the IRA law have expanded the market place and the tax advantages. Some of these later IRAs require employer sponsorship before they may be established. Others may be established solely by the individual, providing eligibility requirements are met. Each offers unique tax advantages that appeal to a variety of individuals.

**Note: The purpose of the following information is to provide a broad overview of the IRA. I recommend reviewing IRS Publication 590-A and 590-B for complete details, contribution limits, and eligibility requirements for the Traditional IRA and the Roth IRA, since provisions of the law are complex and subject to change. I also recommend reviewing IRS Publication 560 for complete details, contribution limits, and eligibility requirements for the SEP IRA and the SIMPLE IRA. These publications are found at www.irs.gov.**

## THE DIFFERENT TYPES OF IRAs

I will center this discussion on the Traditional IRA and the Roth IRA, since these are the types of IRAs used in self-directed IRAs. Mention is made of the SEP IRA and SIMPLE IRA since they contain the acronym IRA and are employer-sponsored plans. These plans are likely to be self-directed in very small, family-owned businesses. The i401(k) is outlined also, since it is a type of individual plan like an IRA and likely to be self-directed; although in fact, it is an employer-sponsored plan for business owners with no employees.

## THE TRADITIONAL IRA

The Traditional IRA which is also called an "ordinary" IRA or a "regular" IRA allows individuals with earned income for the tax year and who have not yet reached age 70½ to make tax-deductible contributions into an account.

In 2015, a contribution of $5,500.00 may be made by an individual below age 50; if the individual is age 50 or older, a catch-up provision allows for a $6,500.00 contribution. Note the amount of the contribution is determined by the amount of the individual's earned income for that tax year. So, if the individual's earned income is less than $5,500.00

(below age 50) or less than $6,500.00 (age 50 and above), the individual may contribute only up to a maximum of his/her earned income for that tax year.

Generally speaking, these contributions are tax deductible when certain other eligibility requirements are met. Other eligibility requirements pertain to marital status, the individual's tax-filing status, the total amount of *modified* adjusted gross income shown on the income-tax return, and whether or not an individual or spouse (if applicable) is covered by an employer-sponsored retirement plan. The deductibility of these contributions is phased out contingent on the above-referenced factors; however, non-deductible contributions may be permitted into the Traditional IRA. All contributions must be made by the tax-filing deadline of April 15th in the following year.

Since eligibility requirements depend on the foregoing factors, it is not uncommon for accountants to suggest Traditional IRA contributions during tax-filing season as a means of reducing the amount of income tax an individual (and/or spouse) may have to pay. If the taxpayer has funds available to make the IRA contribution by the filing deadline of April 15, some or all of the IRA contribution may be recouped once a tax refund check is received.

Distributions

Assets in the IRA grow on a tax-deferred basis; this means there is no income tax payable on any of the growth in the account. The income tax is applied when the IRA owner takes distributions. Distributions are subject to income tax, since the contributions into the account were tax deductible when made. (If any of the contributions were not tax deductible, these contributions are distributed income-tax free.) If the IRA owner takes a distribution before age 59½, the distribution is subject to a penalty tax of 10%, as well as income tax, unless the distribution qualifies as an exception.

The exceptions to this early withdrawal provision may occur if the distributions are used for unreimbursed medical expenses; medical insurance due to a period of unemployment; for total and permanent disability; for the beneficiary of an inherited IRA; for an annuity; for qualified higher education expenses; for buying, building, or rebuilding a first home; for an IRS levy of the qualified plan; and for a qualified reservist distribution. I recommend consulting with a tax attorney for the complex details associated with each exception.

By the time the IRA owner attains the age of 70½, it is necessary for minimum distributions to begin. These distributions are called "required minimum distributions" and are referred to as RMDs; they are based upon the IRA owner's age and marital status, the beneficiary's age, and life expectancies. Again, if the IRA owner does not take distributions when required, there is a rather high penalty tax of 50% assessed on the amount which should have been distributed.

Inherited Traditional IRA

The Traditional IRA may be inherited by whomever the owner has named to receive benefits; this is referred to as the beneficiary of the IRA. In situations wherein other than a spouse is named to inherit the IRA as its beneficiary, the account is retitled to reflect this. Let's say the owner of the IRA, John Adams, passes away. The account is retitled "Sunwest Trust Custodian for Jane Adams Brown Inherited IRA as Beneficiary for John Adams." This is done since money cannot be distributed from a dead person's account.

If only the spouse is named to receive benefits, the spouse can either assume ownership of that account; "roll" (move) that account into his/her own IRA; or may continue to remain as beneficiary.

If the spouse assumes ownership of the Traditional IRA, then his/her age is used to determine the start of required minimum distributions.

Alternatively, when the spouse remains as beneficiary of the Traditional IRA, then required minimum distributions on the account begin in the year the deceased would have become age 70½.

If the IRA owner dies at age 70½ or later after required minimum distributions have started, distributions continue. These distributions are based upon whichever age (either the spouse beneficiary's age or what would have been the deceased owner's age in the year following death) results in the longer pay out.

If another individual(s) or entity is named beneficiary, then a set of required minimum distribution rules apply in the year following the deceased owner's death, ranging from using the IRA owner's age, the beneficiary's age, and/or alternately a five-year pay out.

Generally speaking, all distributions are treated as taxable income when received, and if the required minimum distribution is not taken, then a 50% penalty tax applies to the amount that should have been distributed.

Prohibited Transactions

The Traditional IRA's tax-advantaged status can be forfeited if the account is used improperly for a prohibited transaction by the IRA owner, beneficiary, or any disqualified person. Disqualified persons are identified as the fiduciary on the account, and certain members of the family, such as the IRA owner's spouse, ancestor (which means parents, grand-parents, etc., of the owner), lineal descendants of the owner (which means children, grandchildren, etc.) and spouses of those lineal descendants.

For example, a prohibited transaction would occur if any of the above-described individuals borrow money from the IRA; sell property to the IRA; use the IRA as security for a loan; or buy property for either present or future use using IRA funds. These are examples of just a few of the prohibited transactions.

If a prohibited transaction occurs, the entire IRA is distributed; and the full distribution (except for any non-deductible contributions) is taxable as income. Depending on the age of the IRA owner, the distribution may be subject to the 10% early distribution tax, as well.

## THE ROTH IRA

The Roth IRA was created through the Tax Payer Relief Act of 1997 and allows individuals to establish a different type of IRA that is less restrictive than the Traditional IRA.

The Roth IRA permits individuals who satisfy eligibility requirements to make after-tax contributions into a Roth IRA. Eligibility is determined by the individual's marital status, tax-filing status, and the total amount of *modified* adjusted gross income shown on the income-tax return. Depending on the tax-filing status, if the individual's *modified* adjusted gross income is above a particular amount, a Roth IRA may not be set up. Unlike the Traditional IRA, the individual's age does not play a part in whether or not the Roth IRA may be established.

In 2015, contributions of $5,500.00 may be made by individuals below age 50; if the individual is age 50 or older, a catch-up provision allows for a $6,500.00 contribution. As with the Traditional IRA, the contribution amount is limited to the amount of earned income the individual has for that tax year. So, if the individual's earned income is less than $5,500.00 (below age 50) or less than $6,500.00 (age 50 and above), the individual may contribute only up to a maximum of his/her earned income for that tax year.

The amount of the Roth contribution may be reduced further based upon the individual's placement within a range of *modified* adjusted-gross-income amounts. Consideration is also given as to whether or not the individual makes a contribution into a Traditional IRA. In effect, if the individual is below age 50 and wants to make contributions to both types of IRAs, the total amount of the contributions may not exceed $5,500.00, which may be reduced further by the individual's placement within a range of *modified* adjusted-gross-income amounts. All contributions must be made by the tax-filing deadline of April 15$^{th}$ in the following year.

Distributions

Any growth on the assets inside the account is tax free, and there is no age by which the IRA owner must start taking distributions from the account. As a matter of fact, since after-tax dollars are used, the IRA owner may take distribution of those after-tax contributions at any time.

Regarding the balance of the Roth IRA which could represent growth on assets or un-taxed dollars, the IRA owner may take these distributions income-tax free, providing the distributions are *qualified*.

Generally speaking, distributions are considered *qualified* if the IRA owner is at least age 59½ and the account is established for five years. In addition, an owner's total and permanent disability; a beneficiary inheriting the IRA; and the buying, building, or rebuilding of a first home are considered *qualified* distributions, as well, if the account is established for five years.

If a nonqualified distribution is made, the growth on assets is subject to income tax and a penalty tax of 10%, unless the nonqualified distribution qualifies as an exception.

The exceptions to this nonqualified distribution provision may occur if the distributions are used for: unreimbursed medical expenses; medical insurance due to a period of unemployment; qualified higher education expenses; an IRS levy of the qualified plan; and a qualified reservist distribution. I recommend consulting with a tax attorney for the complex details associated with each exception.

Inherited Roth IRA

The Roth IRA may be inherited by whomever the owner has named to receive benefits; this is referred to as the beneficiary of the IRA. After the Roth IRA owner's death, however, required minimum distribution rules are applied to the Roth assets held by the beneficiary.

In situations wherein other than the spouse is named to inherit the IRA as its beneficiary, the account is retitled to reflect this. Let's say the owner of the IRA, John Adams, passes away. The account is retitled "Sunwest Trust Custodian for Jane Adams Brown Inherited IRA as Beneficiary for John Adams." This is done since money cannot be distributed from a dead person's account.

If only the spouse is named to receive benefits, the spouse can either assume ownership of that account; "roll" (move) that account into his/her own Roth IRA; or may continue to remain as beneficiary.

In situations where the spouse remains as beneficiary of the Roth IRA and the owner died before age 70½, then required minimum distributions on the account begin in the year the deceased would have become age 70½.

If another individual(s) or entity is named beneficiary, then a set of required minimum distribution rules apply in the year following the deceased owner's death, ranging from using the IRA owner's age and/or the beneficiary's age, and/or a mandatory five-year pay out.

All distributions from the Roth IRA are income-tax free, if the account had been established for five years.

In all instances regarding required minimum distributions upon the death of the Roth IRA owner, if the required minimum distribution is not taken, then the 50% penalty tax applies to the amount that should have been distributed.

Prohibited Transactions

The Roth IRA's tax-advantaged status can be forfeited if the account is used improperly for a prohibited transaction by the IRA owner, beneficiary, or any disqualified person. Disqualified persons are identified as the fiduciary on the account, and certain members of the family, such as the IRA owner's spouse, ancestor (which means parents, grand-parents, etc., of the owner), lineal descendants of the owner (which means children, grandchildren, etc.) and spouses of those lineal descendants.

For example, a prohibited transaction would occur if any of the above-described individuals borrow money from the IRA; sell property to the IRA; use the IRA as security for a loan; or buy property using IRA funds for either present or future use. These are examples of just a few of the prohibited transactions.

If that occurs, the account ceases being an IRA and all of its assets are distributed. If the owner is below 59½, this is a nonqualified distribution and the un-taxed growth on the assets is subject to income tax and a penalty tax of 10%.

## ROLLOVER CONTRIBUTIONS

In general, IRA owners and participants of employer-sponsored retirement plans may take a distribution from an account before age 59½, and it will not be taxed as an early distribution nor subject to a penalty tax, providing certain guidelines are met. This is called a *rollover*, and the amount of the distribution must be rolled over into another IRA or an eligible employer-sponsored retirement plan within a 60-day period.

There are some exceptions to this rule and an IRA owner may apply for a waiver from taxation and the penalty tax under the following situations: errors made by the financial institution handling the rollover; the owner's death, disability, hospitalization, or incarceration; a foreign power imposing restrictions on the owner; and/or a postal error.

If an IRA owner desires to roll a distribution from one IRA into another IRA, the owner is limited to one tax-free rollover per 12-month period within a timeframe that begins on the date of distribution. This is true regardless of the number of IRA accounts held by the owner and includes any Traditional IRAs, Roth IRAs, SEP-IRAs, and SIMPLE IRAs.

On the other hand, there is no limit to the number of direct rollovers or custodian-to-custodian transfers per year that may be made into a Traditional IRA from other eligible employer-sponsored retirement plans. Although SEP-IRAs and SIMPLE IRAs are employer-sponsored plans, they are excluded from this provision.

If the owner of a Traditional IRA wants to roll a distribution into a Roth IRA, this is called a *conversion* and the number of conversions an owner may make is not limited. Conversions are covered next.

## CONVERSION CONTRIBUTIONS

Generally speaking, a conversion occurs when an owner moves part or all of the assets from a Traditional IRA or an eligible employer-sponsored retirement plan, including SEP-IRA and SIMPLE IRA, into a Roth IRA. As with rollovers, the assets must be converted within a 60-day period.

In effect, the owner is moving assets that would be subject to income tax upon distribution into an account that may distribute assets on an income-tax free basis. With conversions, the owner pays income taxes at the time of conversion.

Any conversion contribution amounts in the Roth IRA must stay in the account at least five years from the year of deposit, before they may be withdrawn penalty-tax free, assuming the Roth IRA owner is at least 59 ½ at the time of withdrawal.

## SEP-IRA

Another type of IRA is a Simplified Employee Pension (SEP), known as a SEP-IRA; this account requires an employer/employee relationship. This type of account was established by the Revenue Act of 1978. In this arrangement, the employer sets up Traditional IRAs for each employee, and the employee owns and controls the IRA. The employer makes contributions directly into the employees' accounts and may not place any restrictions on the accounts. An owner employee is eligible to participate in this plan.

The employer must make contributions for all employees based on a written formula; and interestingly enough, contributions may be made to employee participants age 70½ and older.

In 2015, the contribution limit is based upon 25% of the employee's compensation or $53,000.00, whichever is less. The amount used for employee compensation is capped at $265,000.00 in this formula. If the employer contributes to another type of employees' qualified retirement plan in addition to the SEP-IRA, the combined contribution limit among the plans is capped at the lesser of 25% of the employee's compensation or $53,000.00. The employer receives a deduction within certain IRS limits for the amount paid out in employee contributions. Employer contribution amounts are not shown on the employees' W-2s.

Except as previously noted regarding contributions above age 70½, all of the rules pertaining to the Traditional IRA apply to the SEP-IRA.

### SIMPLE-IRA

A SIMPLE-IRA is a Savings Incentive Match Plan for Employees (SIMPLE). This is an employer-sponsored plan which may be established if the employer has 100 or fewer employees. This type of account was established by the Small Business Protection Act of 1996. Under this plan, the employer sets up Traditional IRAs for all employees who want to participate in the plan. Employees participate by making contributions that reduce their salaries. An owner employee is eligible to participate in this plan.

In 2015, an employee may make a contribution up to $12,500.00 via salary reduction; if an employee is age 50 or older, the amount of the reduction may be up to $15,500.00 pursuant to the catch-up provision. An employee may not contribute more than total compensation, however. If an employee also contributes to another employer-sponsored plan, the total amount of employee contributions among all the plans is capped at $18,000.00.

In the SIMPLE-IRA, generally, the employer matches the employees' contributions on a dollar-for-dollar basis up to 3% of employee compensation.

The employer receives a deduction for the amount paid out in employee contributions. The employees' salary reductions are made with pre-tax dollars, and the employer contributions are not included on the employees' W-2s as compensation.

Rules applicable to the Traditional IRA apply; however, the early withdrawal penalty increases from 10% to 25% if the employee is below age 59½ and funds are withdrawn within two years of account set up.

## i401(k)

An i401(k) is not an IRA; but since it covers only one individual (or perhaps two in spousal situations) and may be self-directed, it is mentioned in this chapter.

An i401(k) is actually an employer-sponsored traditional 401(k) retirement plan that is designed to cover an individual business owner who has no employees, or just the business owner and his or her spouse. The i401(k) is also known as a "solo 401(k)" or a "solo (k)." The business owner may operate as a corporation, a Subchapter S corporation, a partnership, a limited liability company, or a sole proprietor. This type of account was established by the Economic Growth and Tax Relief Reconciliation Act of 2001.

In this plan, the business owner is the employer and also the employee; and contributions are made by both. The employee's contributions are called deferrals. In 2015, the amount the employee may contribute in deferrals is 100% of compensation or $18,000.00, whichever is less. If the employee is age 50 or older, the catch-up provision allows up to a $24,000.00 contribution. These deferrals are made with pre-tax dollars. Note that a Roth account may be set up as part of the plan, and after-tax deferrals may be made into that designated Roth account.

Limits on these deferrals are on a per individual basis; so if the owner is participating in another employer-sponsored retirement plan, these amounts must be coordinated.

There is a limit on the amount the employer may contribute to the employee's account, as well. In 2015, the amount the employer may contribute depends on the type of business entity under which it operates and may be up to 25% of the employee's compensation or $53,000.00, whichever is less. The employer receives a deduction within certain IRS limits for the amount paid as employee contributions.

Assets in the account grow on a tax-deferred basis and generally may not be withdrawn before age 59½ without penalty, although there are some exceptions to this rule. Unlike the IRA, the i401(k) also permits the employee to make loans on the account.

In the next chapter, I explore the differences of IRAs with traditional assets and IRAs with non-traditional assets.

Chapter 1

## HIGHLIGHTS FROM CHAPTER 1

- **Contributions to Traditional IRAs are generally tax-deductible.**
- **Distributions from Traditional IRAs are generally subject to income tax.**
- **Contributions to Roth IRAs are made with after-tax dollars.**
- **Distributions from Roth IRAs are generally income-tax free.**
- **Withdrawals before age 59½ from a Traditional IRA are generally taxable and subject to an early distribution penalty of 10%.**
- **A Traditional IRA owner must begin required minimum distributions from the account by age 70½.**
- **A Roth IRA owner does not have to take required minimum distributions.**
- **A rollover distribution must be reinvested into an IRA within 60 days of receipt of the distribution or it will become taxable income.**
- **Only one IRA rollover is permitted per individual per 12-month period.**
- **A conversion to a Roth IRA is income taxable at the time it is made.**
- **SEP-IRAs are Traditional IRAs funded by employers, but owned by the employee.**
- **SIMPLE-IRAs are Traditional IRAs funded by both the employer and the employee, and owned by the employee.**
- **i401(k)s are designed for business owners with no employees.**

## ADDITIONAL RESOURCES

**Sunwest Trust sponsors a channel on www.youtube.com called "sunwestira" in which many of the topics in this chapter are discussed. I recommend viewing the following to augment the information in this chapter.**

- "Differences Between Traditional IRA & Roth IRA-Choosing the Right IRA" November 4, 2014

- "Requirements for IRA Contributions" June 29, 2011

- "Avoid IRA Prohibited Transactions from Internal Revenue Code IRC Section 408m" August 5, 2014

- "Required Minimum Distributions" March 5, 2013

- "Required Minimum Distribution Rules-What You Need to Know" December 2, 2014

- "IRA Distribution Rules: Taking an IRA Distribution After Age 59½" December 18, 2015

- "Age 59½, Can I Use SEP Funds to Buy Personal Residence?" November 24, 2015

- "Pros and Cons of a Roth IRA Conversion—What Taxes Will I Have to Pay?" December 17, 2013

- "IRA to IRA Transfer-401K Direct Rollover IRA & In-Service Distribution" July 8, 2014

- "IRA Rollover vs. Direct Transfer vs. Direct 401K Rollover-Which Is More Advantageous?" July 14, 2014

- "Pros and Cons-Solo 401k Personal Loan Rules" April 16, 2013

# CHAPTER 2

# WHAT IS A SELF-DIRECTED IRA?

Now that the different types of IRAs are identified, let's look at the assets that may be held in them to refine the definition of what is meant by "self-directed." Broadly speaking, all IRAs are self-directed. In this context, an individual makes the choice of which institution holds the IRA and into what types of investments the IRA's contributions are made. Having said that, I want to further refine the definition of Self-Directed IRA as used in this book.

## IRA ASSETS: TRADITIONAL OR NON-TRADITIONAL?

The tax law governing IRAs is rather open ended when it comes to describing what assets may be in an IRA and lists cash and property. It prohibits collectibles, such as artwork, rugs, antiques, metals, gems, stamps, coins, alcoholic beverages, and certain other tangible personal property; life insurance; and stock in Subchapter S corporations.

A good deal of IRA assets are held in mutual funds, money market accounts, stocks, bonds, certificates of deposit, and annuities. These assets, most of which are publicly traded, offer a ready market for liquidity. In this book, this is referred to as an IRA with traditional assets.

As previously mentioned however, the law describing the assets which may be included in an IRA is broad, and an IRA owner may include a variety of assets in the account other than the traditional assets previously described. These types of assets are called non-traditional assets.

Some types of non-traditional assets which may be included are commercial and residential real estate; land; trust deeds; mortgages; private placements; promissory notes; tax liens; selected precious metals such as gold, silver, palladium, and platinum which meet a purity content requirement; C corporation stock; and limited liability companies (LLCs). And, this list is by no means exhaustive.

In this book, an IRA containing non-traditional assets will be referred to as a Self-Directed IRA.

**WHY CONSIDER A SELF-DIRECTED IRA?**

There are several reasons why an individual would consider a Self-Directed IRA.

- An individual may be apprehensive about stock market volatility.
- Rather than place all of the assets in the stock market with high-profile, publicly-traded companies, an individual may want diversification.
- An individual may want to invest locally, perhaps in start-up companies.
- An individual may have much experience in real estate and want to invest in rental property or raw land.
- An individual knows that higher risk could mean higher rewards.

Considering a Self-Directed IRA is one thing; taking the next step to establish one is another. Before establishing a Self-Directed IRA, an individual should assess the retirement goals to be met. Does the individual have a picture or goal of what is to be accomplished? Is there a roadmap to achieve this goal? Will a Self-Directed IRA fit into the overall plan or strategy? Will the beneficiary of the Self-Directed IRA be able to handle the investments, if something happens to the owner?

## SELF-DIRECTED IRAS ARE NOT FOR EVERYONE

Let me begin by saying that a Self-Directed IRA is not for everyone; it is a hands-on account requiring much of the IRA owner's time and talent. Perhaps the easiest way to explain this is to contrast the role of the owner of an IRA funded with traditional assets with the role of the owner of a Self-Directed IRA.

In IRAs holding traditional assets, the owner may play a rather passive role in the operation of the account, more often than not, relying on the institution which holds the IRA.

The institution which holds the IRA is called the trustee for the IRA and is generally a bank or trust company, a federally-insured credit union, a savings and loan, or a brokerage house. The trustee restricts the type of IRA investments it offers and may provide investment advice.

Based upon the choices offered by the institution in which the account is established or by the broker, the IRA owner chooses the type of traditional asset to be placed in the account. Chances are, the IRA owner may review the performance on the account once or twice a year, but does not actively monitor the account to ensure that it is operating within Internal Revenue Code (IRC) guidelines.

In addition to holding the assets in the account, the institution monitors account activity to determine that contributions and transactions are within the guidelines allowed, prepares account valuations, and also sends the Internal Revenue Service (IRS) the required tax forms.

With a Self-Directed IRA, the IRA owner plays an active role. Assets in a Self-Directed IRA are held by the Custodian of the account; the Custodian, acting upon directions from the owner, issues checks to buy assets on behalf of the IRA and furnishes the tax forms to the IRS. Custodians do not provide investment, accounting, or legal advice.

The Self-Directed IRA owner chooses the type of asset in which to invest and does the research necessary to determine if the asset qualifies under IRC guidelines. The responsibility is solely the owner's. The amount of time required depends on the asset involved. The owner monitors that asset on an ongoing basis and is responsible for providing valuations of the asset held within the Self-Directed IRA. The owner also has responsibility to make certain that the IRA does not engage in any prohibited transactions. (Prohibited transactions are covered in detail in Chapter 6.)

Let's move from speaking generally and contrast the realities of owning rental properties in an IRA with traditional assets versus owning rental properties in a Self-Directed IRA.

In the IRA with traditional assets, the owner contacts the broker on the account and indicates the desire to own rental properties to produce an income stream. The broker performs due diligence and suggests a Real Estate Investment Trust (REIT) to the owner.

The REIT is like a mutual fund in that it sells shares in a company that owns or finances income-producing property. REITs own many varieties of rental properties from apartment houses, to hospitals, to shopping centers, to storage centers. The IRA purchases shares in the REIT. The owner meets with the broker twice a year to monitor the performance of all the assets in the IRA and is happy with the arrangement.

In the Self-Directed IRA, the owner who desires a rental property asset contacts a realtor who is a trusted advisor. The owner has performed research for the locale and explains the specifications for the property to be acquired. The realtor finds four properties meeting these specifications, and the owner goes to look at each one of the properties.

Upon deciding on one of the properties, the owner instructs the Custodian to buy the property and title is transferred to the Self-Directed IRA. Each month, the IRA owner monitors the account to make certain the rent check has come in, and drives by the house to see that the property is being kept in good condition. The Self-Directed IRA owner is happy with this arrangement.

## THREE ELEMENTS TO CONSIDER BEFORE MOVING FORWARD

In addition to assessing retirement goals, an individual should look at the following three elements before setting up a Self-Directed IRA. They are money, knowledge, and time.

### Money

A Self-Directed IRA operates more efficiently if an individual has a substantial amount of money in the account. In effect, a younger individual who is just starting out and who may be able to contribute only $5,500.00 into an account, does not have the same investment options as an individual with $30,000.00 already accumulated in the Self-Directed IRA. This accumulation may be the result of contributions, a direct rollover from a previous employer's 401(k) plan, or a custodian-to-custodian transfer. It may be better for the younger individual to accumulate assets in an IRA with traditional assets, and then transfer a substantial amount into a Self-Directed IRA.

In this respect too, there is the Custodian's fee on the Self-Directed IRA to consider. Custodians hold the assets in the Self-Directed IRA for the owner and make their money by charging fees in the administration of the account. Custodians do not sell products; therefore, their income derives from the services provided.

Some Custodians charge a flat annual fee; other Custodians charge a fee as a percentage of assets under management. Let's say for example, the annual fee for a Self-Directed IRA is a flat fee of $225.00. Using $5,500.00 as the scenario, the annual fee amounts to 4.0% of the contribution. This fee would need to be factored in to any return the account generates.

Let's assume the IRA owner finds a non-traditional investment for $5,500.00; and at the end of the year, the return on this investment is 10%. Inasmuch as 4.0% was raked off the top in the form of the fee, the net return to the owner is actually 6.0%. This owner would need to determine if this return makes fiscal sense and is consistent with retirement goals.

On the other hand, if the owner of a Self-Directed IRA with $30,000.00 finds a non-traditional asset in which to invest and earns 10% at the end of the year, that is another story. In our example, the flat fee of $225.00 represents less than

0.75% of the contribution. There is less than 1.0% raked off the top in the form of the fee, and the net investment result is 9.25%. This may make more fiscal sense and may be in line with the owner's retirement goals.

Note that the fee charged by a custodian may be paid out side of the IRA. Even so, I believe the fee still plays a part in factoring the return on the investment.

Knowledge/Experience and/or Expertise

The ability to invest in non-traditional assets is attractive to the owner of a Self-Directed IRA; but I recommend that the owner possess knowledge or experience in the particular field of the investment before moving forward. An owner may think an investment offering a high return in a tech start-up company and of which he/she does not possess knowledge, is the asset to place in the IRA. Often, this is a recipe for disaster since the expected return does not materialize. An informed or knowledgeable investor of the industry may have known that this was a high-risk type of investment and may have been wary of what to expect.

An example of a popular non-traditional asset is rental properties and this type of asset may be ideal for realtors. Realtors have knowledge of neighborhoods, housing, schools, and resale value of properties. If an owner wants to invest in real estate, but does not have the knowledge or experience, the owner may affiliate with a realtor who does.

The point is that the owner of a Self-Directed IRA should not proceed blindly in making investment choices, but should have the knowledge or experience to back up the investment choices. In lieu of the owner's direct knowledge or experience, I recommend working with a trusted advisor on the subject investment.

Time

Time is a key factor to the owner of a Self-Directed IRA, because it is the owner's responsibility to be directly involved in the choosing and the management of the IRA's assets. This responsibility requires an investment of time.

The Self-Directed IRA owner plays a key role in the operation of this account. It is the owner who researches the investments to determine that they are legitimate and that the provider can be trusted; and it is the owner who determines if the investment complies with IRC guidelines. It is the owner who provides valuations to the Custodian so that the required IRS tax forms may be prepared and sent on time. Finally, it is the owner who could ultimately lose money if the investment fails or who pays additional taxes for noncompliance.

Another aspect of time is the following. If the individual does not have a large amount with which to set up the Self-Directed IRA, a larger sum may be accumulated over time. Likewise, knowledge or experience of a particular type of investment may be acquired over time.

If the individual has money and knowledge, but doesn't have the time, a trusted advisor may be hired by the individual to invest the time required for a Self-Directed IRA.

## ALL EGGS IN ONE BASKET?

The quote "don't put all your eggs in one basket" is familiar to all; and the same holds true for a Self-Directed IRA. A Self-Directed IRA should be thought of as a diversification tool. And, since the tax code permits individuals to own a number of IRAs, an owner would be wise to keep an IRA with traditional assets, as well.

While it is true that Self-Directed IRAs may provide a higher than average return, it is also true that they may be higher risk than an IRA with traditional assets. It is important to recognize that an IRA may be the largest asset an individual owns and the basis for funding his/her retirement. The investment return on IRA assets can impact the individual's lifestyle in retirement years.

In the next chapter, I provide some tips in setting up a Self-Directed IRA.

## HIGHLIGHTS FROM CHAPTER 2

- An IRA with traditional assets generally holds mutual funds, money market accounts, stocks, bonds, certificates of deposit, and annuities.
- A Self-Directed IRA may hold assets that are not traded publicly on any exchange.
- Self-Directed IRAs are not for everyone and an individual needs to ascertain if this type of IRA is consistent with retirement goals.
- An IRA may not invest in collectibles, such as artwork, rugs, antiques, metals, gems, stamps, coins, alcoholic beverages, and certain other tangible personal property; life insurance; and stock in S corporations.
- Self-Directed IRAs may offer a higher return than an IRA with traditional assets; however, there may be a higher risk associated with a Self-Directed IRA.
- Self-Directed IRAs may require a larger time commitment by the owner than an IRA with traditional assets.
- An individual who wants to open a Self-Directed IRA is wise to maintain an IRA with traditional assets, as well.
- Three elements to consider before opening a Self-Directed IRA are money, knowledge/experience, and time.

Chapter 2

## ADDITIONAL RESOURCES

**Sunwest Trust sponsors a channel on www.youtube.com called "sunwestira" in which many of the topics in this chapter are discussed. I recommend viewing the following to augment the information in this chapter.**

- "Establishing Retirement Goals for Your IRA" January 13, 2015

- "Is a Self-Directed IRA a Good Idea for You?" January 20, 2015

- "Difference Between Brokerage IRA and Self-Directed IRA" May 5, 2015

- "Invest in a Business With an IRA-It Starts With the Right IRA" May 12, 2015

- "Three Elements to Starting a Self-Directed IRA" September 15, 2015

- "Sunwest Trust Reviews—Client Interview and Testimonial" November 16, 2015

The Self-Directed IRA Handbook
by Mat Sorensen, Attorney at Law

# CHAPTER 3

# TIPS ON SETTING UP A SELF-DIRECTED IRA

As mentioned in the previous chapter, the Self-Directed IRA owner makes the investment decisions on the account, but this should not be done in a vacuum. I recommend a team approach of professionals for the individual who desires to set up a Self-Directed IRA. This team can make certain the IRA owner does not invest inadvertently in an item that could be a prohibited transaction or a fraudulent investment.

There may be some up-front costs with lining up the team, but it is my opinion that this will save money in the long run. It will also allow for the efficient operation of the Self-Directed IRA. The team members I would assemble follow.

## THE TEAM

### Attorney

An attorney may give valuable advice regarding tax planning to the IRA owner. The IRA owner may ask the attorney to review any documents related to investments to determine any problems with the language therein and the law which governs IRAs. If the owner wishes to establish an IRA

Limited Liability Company (IRA-LLC), the attorney is instrumental in drawing up the agreement. Also, an attorney may counsel an IRA owner on the prohibited transaction rules.

## Accountant

An accountant should have current knowledge of contribution limits and any required tax filings if there are C corporations, limited liability companies, limited partnerships, or debt held by the IRA. Also, an accountant can advise an IRA owner on the prohibited transaction rules.

## Fee-Based Financial Advisor

A financial advisor is skilled in financial planning and may assist an IRA owner in outlining an overall financial plan to help achieve the owner's retirement goals. The financial adviser can determine if a proposed investment fits into the overall retirement plan.

Since the financial advisor is fee based, there is no product for sale or commission involved and the advice given should be totally objective. The National Association of Personal Financial Advisors at www.napfa.org provides information for financial advisors in the IRA owner's locale. In my opinion, the financial advisor is the most important member on the team.

## Realtor/Broker

Unless the IRA owner happens to be a realtor, if the IRA owner wants rental property, commercial property, or land to be held in the IRA, it is a good idea to work with a realtor. This team member can be of service later on, too, by providing market analyses, and "comps" for the valuations of the property held. Valuations are required on an annual basis in a Self-Directed IRA.

### Precious-Metals Broker

If the IRA owner wants to put precious metals in the IRA, it is important to find a reputable precious-metals broker with whom to do business, and who understands the storage requirements for precious metals held within a Self-Directed IRA.

### Investment Broker or Sponsor

If the IRA owner wants a special type of investment such as a business start-up or private placement, the IRA owner will want to engage the services of an investment broker or sponsor. It is important for the IRA owner to have an understanding of how this type of investment will work, how the investment makes a profit, how the broker or sponsor gets paid, and what eventually is going to be passed on to the IRA.

### Custodian

A custodian is an entity that is governed by Section 408(n) of the Internal Revenue Code and is qualified to hold the assets of the Self-Directed IRA. The custodian does not offer any products, nor does it provide legal, accounting, or investment advice. The key focus here is whether or not the custodian will handle the assets the IRA owner is contemplating.

## BUYER BEWARE...WHO IS A CUSTODIAN?

I encourage you to be diligent. Having done searches on the internet, I have found information, articles, and advertisements listed by persons or entities purporting to set up IRAs; and I want to summarize the five general categories of persons or entities I have found. All have a role to play, but ultimately an individual who wants to set up a Self-Directed IRA will need to have a custodian that holds title to the assets as required by IRC Section 408(n).

Investment Seller or Creator of the Investment

These persons or entities are the creators of the investment and are looking for individuals who will loan money to them for the promise of a return. It may even be a neighbor who flips houses and is looking for someone who may be able to finance this arrangement. Creators of investments may sell their investments to be held in IRAs or outside of IRAs. If the individual wants to place this asset in an IRA, a custodian is required to hold the asset.

Promoter or Broker

These persons or entities do not create investments, but try to raise money for an investment that has been created and which is not necessarily their own. Perhaps they want to raise money for oil and gas investments; they are not actually the entity doing the drilling, but are raising money for the entity that is doing the drilling. After the investment is sold, the promoter or broker generally moves on and the individual has no more interaction with them. If the individual wants to place an asset sold by a promoter or broker into an IRA, a custodian is required to hold the asset.

Limited Liability Company (LLC) Creators

There are sites that offer the ability to create a limited liability company (LLC) to enable checkbook control of the IRA. These persons or entities actually establish the LLC and even may help the individual set up an account with a custodian to hold the LLC, but they are not a custodian. The individual will need to research the custodian in this affiliation to determine whether or not this is the custodian with whom to do business.

Third Party Administrator (TPA)

Third Party Administrators are the unregulated record-keeping companies that record the activity on the account and send the appropriate tax forms to the IRS. TPAs must be affiliated with a custodian. TPAs do not hold the assets of the IRA; this is the function of a custodian.

Custodian

Internal Revenue Code Section 408(n) defines a custodian for the purposes of holding an IRA as an entity that is governed by state banking regulations and is supervised and examined by the state's Banking Commissioner; it adheres to the banking laws of its state of domicile. A custodian holds title to the assets in a Self-Directed IRA.

**SELECTING A CUSTODIAN**

After assembling a team of advisors and performing research on custodians, the next step for an individual who desires to proceed with setting up a Self-Directed IRA is to select a custodian.

The custodian plays a key role in an individual's Self-Directed IRA, since it limits the type of assets it will hold. A number of custodians will not hold title to the non-traditional assets that are discussed in this book. An individual will want to make certain that the types of investments he/she desires to place in the Self-Directed IRA are handled by the custodian.

As Henry Ford, the creator of the Ford Motor Company said, "Any customer can have a car painted any colour he wants, so long as it is black." The individual will do well to determine that he/she does not end up with a black car, when something else is desired!

It is possible that one of the trusted advisors may recommend a custodian or perhaps a friend or associate has a recommendation. The internet has opened all kinds of research opportunities and it is possible to find custodians by conducting a search. A good resource for finding a custodian is the Retirement Industry Trust Association membership directory. This is found at www.RITAUS.org.

I also recommend the individual check the history of the custodian and its ranking with the Better Business Bureau. It is noted that the custodian need not be in the individual's state of residence. Most custodians are able to operate all over the United States. If choosing an out-of-state custodian, the individual will want to check the hours of operation, particularly with time zone differences, to ensure communication compatibility.

## WHY DO CUSTODIANS CHARGE FEES?

Note, regardless of the entity, whether it is a bank, a brokerage house, or a custodian, if the entity is holding an IRA, it is charging a fee of some sort; it just may not be obvious.

Let's take a look at a bank for example. Banks offer certificates of deposit (CDs) to be held in an IRA. Most banks set a minimum amount that may be used to set up the IRA and this could be viewed as a fee. The bank has the use of the money while the money is deposited and this use of the money may be viewed as a fee. If the individual moves the money out of the CD before the CD matures, the investor does not receive the promised rate. This may be viewed as a fee.

When a brokerage house sets up an IRA, there are account maintenance and closing fees. Depending on the assets owned within the IRA, there are service fees. The stocks and bonds may have commissions associated with them. The mutual funds may have management fees associated with them.

Let's say the individual buys a "no-load" mutual fund. In that case, the fee appears in the rate of return the individual is able to earn. Generally speaking, the fee is deducted from the actual rate of return before a declared rate of return is passed on to the individual. In addition, there are fees for other services, such as wire transfers.

Custodians for Self-Directed IRAs charge fees and this may be confusing to some individuals, especially when the IRA owner is managing the account. I remind you that custodians are regulated entities and there is a cost associated with that. Further, custodians do not offer products nor do they recommend investments. They provide services and the required tax reporting; and they hold the assets of a Self-directed IRA. The fees are not hidden; this is how custodians make their money.

In determining the right custodian, it is important to look at the custodian with regard to the type of assets the individual wishes to place in the IRA and to pay close attention to the entire fee schedule. Some custodians charge a flat fee on the account, regardless of the amount of assets held.

Other custodians charge a flat fee for each asset held or the type of asset held, while still others charge a percentage of the value of the account. Note, too, that some of the fee schedules are shown on a quarterly basis, rather than on an annual basis. This will need to be factored in to the decision.

In addition to the annual fee for the account, there is generally an application fee, as well as a fee to close out the account. In the interim, there are transaction fees and the frequency with which they are charged. Most custodians establish a required minimum balance of cash to be maintained in the account to cover contingencies. There is not a standard fee schedule in the industry, so it is important that the individual conduct all the research necessary to make an informed decision.

If the IRA service provider is not regulated by a state or federal entity, it is probably a third-party administrator (TPA) and not a custodian. It will be necessary to determine with which custodian the TPA is affiliated, where the custodian is located, who regulates the custodian, and how long it has been in business. Further, the fees for the custodian may be buried in the fees charged by the TPA, and the individual will want to determine if the fee schedule is attractive. Remember, it is the custodian who will hold the assets of the Self-Directed IRA; the TPA is only the record keeper.

## COMPLETING AN APPLICATION PACKAGE

The next step in establishing a Self-Directed IRA is completing an application; many custodians permit this to be done on line and will accept electronic signatures. Although applications may be completed on line, some custodians require the original signature on the application and require the completed application to be mailed to the custodian.

Further, every custodian will require an acceptable form of government-issued identification, such as a driver's license or a passport. This requirement may necessitate the individual mailing a clear copy of the item, if the individual is unable to scan and electronically transfer the identification with an electronic application.

Walking through the application process may be a little daunting; and at this point, the individual will want to have decided on the type of IRA (Traditional, Roth, SEP, or SIMPLE) to be set up. In addition, the individual will be asked to name the beneficiary on the account at the time of application.

There is generally a place to name a primary beneficiary(ies) and a contingent beneficiary(ies). The primary beneficiary(ies) is listed as the first person(s) to inherit the IRA. If the primary beneficiary(ies) is not alive at the IRA owner's death, the contingent beneficiary or beneficiaries inherit the IRA.

Whenever more than one individual is named as the primary or contingent beneficiary(ies), the individual will need to establish the percentage that each is to inherit. These percentages must add up to 100%. If the individual setting up the IRA is married and does not name the spouse as a beneficiary, the spouse will also have to sign off on this arrangement.

The plan agreement and financial disclosure are also part of the application. The plan agreement details all of the restrictions on the contributions to the account; the required minimum distributions; and discusses inherited IRAs with the required minimum distribution rules for the benefiiaries. Note that the plan agreement and financial disclosure are not the same between custodians and can limit the type of approved investments that are acceptable to be held by the custodian.

Although custodians may draft their own plan agreement and request IRS approval for the document, it is common for custodians to use already-approved IRS plan documents that allow for the type of investments they want to hold, such as non-traditional assets. The plan agreement outlines the expectations of the custodian and the responsibilities of the owner.

Prohibited transactions are summarized in the plan agreement. I have restated the prohibited transactions here. The owner is asked to review the complex prohibited transaction section of the tax code and its attendant tax penalties.

A prohibited transaction is improper use of the IRA by the owner, the beneficiary, or a disqualified person. Disqualified persons are a class of people who include the fiduciary, the owner's spouse, ancestors, lineal descendants, and their spouses. The following are examples of prohibited IRA transactions: borrowing money from the IRA; selling property to the IRA; receiving any compensation for managing the IRA; using the IRA as security for a loan; and buying property for current personal use or for future use with IRA funds. (Prohibited transactions are covered in detail in Chapter 6.)

The financial disclosure outlines the rules that govern the type of IRA that has been established. This section informs that an individual may cancel his/her IRA within seven days of setting it up and have the full contribution returned. There are details regarding the excise penalties assessed for premature distributions which are distributions before age 59½ and the penalty tax when required minimum distributions (if applicable) are not made by age 70½. There are examples and scenarios to assist in the understanding of these rules.

## Fee Disclosure

Part of the application includes the fee disclosure and this is where the fees are shown for submitting the application, the annual fee, the transaction fees and when they may apply, and the minimum cash balance requirements.

## Transfer to a Successor Custodian

If the individual wants to transfer an existing IRA into a Self-Directed IRA, there is generally a transfer form from one IRA to the other which needs to be signed by the account owner, and the custodian to whom the funds are going.

## Hold Harmless Agreement and Disclosure

This agreement outlines the responsibilities of the custodian and the owner of the account. It spells out that the IRA owner is the one making the investment decisions in the purchase of assets for the Self-Directed IRA and that the custodian does not provide investment advice. If the IRA owner loses money on the investment, it is entirely the owner's responsibility. Depending on the agreement, there is often an arbitration clause included.

It is important that an individual read and discuss this agreement and disclosure with an attorney prior to establishing the Self-Directed IRA. It is imperative that the individual knows that all investment decisions, gains and/or losses are entirely his/her responsibility.

## Instruction for Investment

By completing this form, the IRA owner tells the custodian what to purchase for the account and what to liquidate for the account. The custodian does not take any action on the account unless so directed by the IRA owner with this form.

<u>Proper Identification</u>

Generally speaking, the individual must furnish a copy of a valid driver's license or a valid passport to set up an account, pursuant to the USA Patriot Act to ensure that the individual is the person stated in the application. This requirement may necessitate an individual mailing a clear copy of the item, if the individual is unable to scan and electronically transfer the identification with the application.

In the next chapter, I examine the depth of the IRA owner's role in managing the account.

## HIGHLIGHTS FROM CHAPTER 3

- Assemble a team of professionals before setting up a Self-Directed IRA.
- The team of professionals should include an attorney, an accountant, a fee-based financial advisor, a custodian, and depending on the investments the owner desires to place in the IRA, a realtor, a precious-metals broker, and an investment broker or sponsor.
- There are persons and entities purporting themselves to set up IRAs who are not necessarily custodians. The individual needs to be diligent.
- Not all custodians handle non-traditional assets such as real estate, precious metals, or non-publicly traded assets.
- Custodians for Self-Directed IRAs are governed by state banking regulations and supervised by the state's banking commissioner.
- All custodians charge fees and there is not an industry standard among custodians' fees.
- An individual needs to review fees carefully and in light of the type of assets to be placed in the Self-Directed IRA, since some custodians charge on a per-asset basis, and some charge a different fee depending on the asset.
- The type of IRA (Traditional, Roth, SEP, or SIMPLE) to be set up is requested at the time of application.
- If the individual does not name the spouse as beneficiary on the application, the spouse has to sign off on this.
- The plan agreement and financial disclosure

**which are part of the application package outline the types of investments the custodian will hold.**

## ADDITIONAL RESOURCES

**Sunwest Trust sponsors a channel on www.youtube.com called "sunwestira" in which many of the topics in this chapter are discussed. I recommend viewing the following to augment the information in this chapter.**

- "Tips on Setting Up a Self-Directed IRA" March 24, 2015

- "Information About Self-Directed IRAs-Top Resources" April 14, 2015

- "Who Should I Open a Self-Directed IRA With?" November 25, 2014

- "IRA Retirement Planning Information-Are Your Sources Trustworthy?" April 21, 2015

- "Self-Directed IRA Custodian Fees-Why Are They Charged?" October 21, 2015

- "IRA Custodian Fee Comparison-Types of IRA Custodian Fees Explained" November 18, 2014

- "Application Form" January 20, 2015

- "Choosing a Beneficiary for Your Self-Directed IRA-Primary and Contingent" January 17, 2015

- "Transfer Form" January 20, 2015

- "Direction of Investment Form" March 19, 2015

The Self-Directed IRA Handbook
by Mat Sorensen, Attorney at Law

Websites affiliated with Mat Sorensen
- SDIRA Handbook.com

- KKOS Lawywers.com

Other Websites:

- Retirement Industry Trust Association

- RITAUS.org/Membership-Directory

- National Association of Personal Financial Advisors

- www.napfa.org

- www.self-directed-retirement.org/investor-resources

# CHAPTER 4

# THE ROLE OF THE IRA OWNER IN A SELF-DIRECTED IRA— INVESTMENT DECISIONS

The owner of a Self-Directed IRA plays a large role in its management; as I mentioned previously, this is a hands-on arrangement.

In this chapter, I want to cover some of the investment responsibilities of which an IRA owner should be aware and may not have experienced, if this is the individual's first experience with a Self-Directed IRA.

In the next chapter, I cover the administrative responsibilities of the IRA owner to include required minimum distributions, providing information for a required tax filing, and informing the beneficiary.

## INVESTMENT DECISIONS

In the Self-Directed IRA, it is necessary for the IRA owner to find investments, property, and/or opportunities in which to invest, and then perform "due diligence." Due diligence is a common term in business and is used frequently by financial advisors and investment brokers to advise clients that a particular investment has been researched and a review conducted.

Simply put, due diligence means that research has been performed to determine that a business or investment is what it claims to be; and there is no adverse information regarding that business or investment in the public domain. In the case of a Self-Directed IRA, the IRA owner is responsible for all due diligence in regard to the investments placed in the IRA.

To review, the following investments are not allowed in a Self-Directed IRA: collectibles, such as artwork, rugs, antiques, metals, gems, stamps, coins, alcoholic beverages, and certain other tangible personal property; life insurance; and stock in Subchapter S corporations. This means that a wide variety of investments are available for the Self-Directed IRA.

In this section, I will identify some resources for the IRA owner to use and also some phrases and/or scenarios for which to be on the lookout. If the IRA owner pursues investment in assets with which he/she has experience or expertise, the individual will start from an advantageous position.

**CONDUCT RESEARCH**

There is a wealth of information on the internet, and I encourage individuals to take advantage of it. If an IRA owner is approached by the investment seller or an investment promoter/broker regarding an opportunity, the IRA owner should perform some research on the internet. There are various internet search engines to use; and if I were presented with an opportunity to invest in a non-publicly traded company or opportunity, I would perform the following searches.

I would search for the name of the company to see the type of business it is, the length of time it has been in operation, the background of the officers, and if there were any adverse information published on the product, the business, or the officers. I would determine if the business is registered with the state and if there is any information on the company with the Better Business Bureau. I would also perform a search on the investment seller and/or the investment promoter/broker to determine any adverse information or publicity.

In addition, I would contact the state's security or fraud division to see if there is any adverse information on the company or the product in the investor's state or the state in which the company is domiciled. Most states require a securities registration of the business if there is to be an offering to the public. If the offering is deemed a security, the person making the offering to the investor is required to be registered with the state and licensed to do business in the state.

Oftentimes, individuals who perpetrate fraud conduct operations in one state, before moving on to another state. A state's security or fraud division would have this information. The state's security or fraud division may even have informational articles and/or videos to help individuals identify the characteristics of fraudulent investments and those who offer them. For example, on the state of New Mexico's Securities' Division page, there is a documentary on "Ponzi Schemes" that is quite informative and another documentary on fraud that shows real stories and real people and the way in which they were duped.

In 2015, the state of Utah enacted a law creating a white-collar crime registry similar to the sex-offender registries that all states have. The bill which authorized the law will identify persons convicted of securities fraud, theft by deception, unlawful dealing of property by a fiduciary, fraudulent insurance, mortgage fraud, communications fraud, or money laundering. As far as I am aware, this is the first such registry in the nation; and it will compile information that is in the public domain in one easy-to-use site.

Another way for an IRA owner to obtain information is by getting together with friends or associates to share investment ideas and experience. It is possible they may have knowledge of a particular investment or stories to share.

## RATES OF RETURN

We are all familiar with the phrase "…if it seems too good to be true, it probably is." I believe IRA owners should take this to heart and act accordingly. While Self-Directed IRAs may have the opportunity to earn higher returns than IRAs with traditional assets, generally speaking, the owner will not want to obtain these higher returns through overly-risky investments.

If an offering is showing consistent, steady returns or a guaranteed return, an IRA owner may want to check further before requesting the custodian to buy this for the Self-Directed IRA. Steady returns should not be confused with an average rate of return. There are several questions to which the IRA owner should determine answers. One of the questions I would ask is who holds the funds? The IRA owner will want to determine if the invested funds are held by a trustee or broker dealer, or if they are held by the investment creator. If they are held by the investment creator, this may be a warning sign.

Regarding the rate of return, the IRA owner will want to understand how the investment is making the return; i.e., what are the factors that could impact the investment's return positively or negatively. If the IRA owner is unclear regarding how the return is made, he/she will want to do more research.

Another question to ask is whether or not the investments are illiquid? Is the IRA owner able to turn this investment into cash if the promised return is not there? Is the IRA owner able to cash out this investment entirely? Is the IRA owner locked in for a period of time before the investment may be cashed out? If an IRA owner is promised a higher rate of return if a larger sum is invested, this may be a warning sign. This is often done in order to make individuals want to invest more money.

I recommend that IRA owners not get overtaken by the potential of the investment. In addition, the IRA owner will want to assess the risk involved. Is there a possibility that the IRA owner could lose all of the money he/she invests? It is best to ask for a detailed, written description of the opportunity.

If the opportunity is positioned as a security, it is prudent for the IRA owner to determine if the individual offering the opportunity is licensed to sell securities in the state. In addition, it is necessary to ascertain how much the individual selling the opportunity is going to make on the transaction. These are all questions for which the IRA owner needs answers before instructing the custodian to make the purchase for the Self-Directed IRA.

## "PONZI" SCHEMES

Let's talk about "Ponzi" schemes. A Ponzi scheme is

characterized as an opportunity to earn monthly rates of return on an investment of dollars. The scheme may say that the money is invested in real estate development, for example, or a group of publicly-traded stocks; when, in fact, there is no underlying investment. The person offering the opportunity holds the money; and in effect, the monthly payouts are generated to the old investors by the new investors brought in to the scheme.

Sometimes, the additional money added by satisfied investors is used to generate their own current monthly payout. As long as money continues to come in for investment, the scheme continues. Generally speaking, these schemes are used to support the lifestyle of the person offering the opportunity.

Ponzi schemes may be prevalent among affinity groups. An affinity group is a group of people who have an organization or a community in common, for example a fraternal or business organization, a religious community, or a country club, to name a few.

Individuals learn that one of their community has invested in the scheme and is pleased with the return, and that makes it easy for the person offering the scheme to get more investors. There is a certain amount of confidence when individuals are told their pastor, doctor, or banker has already invested. We all know the power of a personal referral or a celebrity endorsement.

The rates of return on Ponzi schemes vary. According to The Economist online article "The Madoff Affair, Con of the Century," dated December 18, 2008, the Madoff investment offered a rate of return around 10% which is not necessarily extraordinary. The unusual aspect of the rate of return was that it was consistent, even when the markets were volatile.

In a local Ponzi scheme in Albuquerque, New Mexico, a well-respected individual of the community was the operator of the scheme. This opportunity offered a rate of return between 8% and 35%, according to "Avoiding Investment Fraud: The Doug Vaughan Documentary," prepared by the New Mexico Regulation and Licensing Department and published March 5, 2014. As the monthly rates of return came in, satisfied investors added more money to this investment opportunity.

This documentary also advised that some of the investors in this scheme learned about the opportunity from their banker. The rate of return tended toward the 35% end-of-the-spectrum at the end of the scheme when the person running the scheme was trying to attract new investors. In both Ponzi schemes identified here, many investors lost their total investment.

The rate of return in the Madoff scenario may not be inordinately high; the rate of return in the Vaughan scenario is considerably higher. I want to introduce the thought that an investment rate of return is relative to an individual's experience and perception.

One of our clients informed me that he had lost money on an investment placed in his Self-Directed IRA. Upon hearing this, I asked him what rate of return had been offered. When he told me the rate of return, it seemed high, and I told him as much. He advised me that it didn't seem high to him at all, since he was used to high interest rates.

It seems that this individual was a higher-risk credit risk and was used to paying high interest rates to borrow money. The high rate of return offered to him on his investment just seemed normal or consistent with his own experience.

I encourage owners of Self-Directed IRAs to talk to friends and associates in whom they place their trust and who may have knowledge or experience in the market in which they are investing.

## OTHER INVESTMENT OPPORTUNITIES

There are other phrases or scenarios that may raise a red flag to owners of Self-Directed IRAs. In one situation, an IRA owner may be told that it is necessary to act immediately or he/she will lose the opportunity. This is designed to create urgency and make the IRA owner act imprudently and without due diligence.

If the opportunity is a good deal for the IRA owner today, it will be a good deal for the IRA owner a week from today. This is not to say that in many investments an IRA owner needs to act quickly in order to get in on the investment; the key is not to let other people exert pressure when making an investment decision.

In my opinion, an IRA owner may want to be wary of investing in a company or opportunity touted as having secret methods or breakthrough technology in the creation of a product or service. Oftentimes, a promoter will claim to have insider information regarding the investment. In these scenarios, the promoter may offer to let the IRA owner in, but requests that the information be kept confidential. It should be apparent to the IRA owner that this opportunity may be suspect. Further, it is illegal to trade or invest on insider information.

Another area which should raise concern is if the opportunity is offering risk-free or guaranteed returns. Any time an IRA owner invests, there is a risk. The higher the return on investment, the greater the risk. In a period of market volatility or markets offering lower returns, an IRA owner should ask how the investment creator is going to make this happen or guarantee this return.

A favorite phrase of mine is "custodian-approved investment." I suggest the IRA owner be careful. Custodian-approved does not mean custodian-guaranteed or that the custodian has done due diligence on the investment. If the reader has made it this far in this book, it is apparent that custodians do not give legal, accounting, or investment advice, nor do they sponsor products or services. In effect, this phrase is a contradiction and I encourage IRA owners not to fall prey to this.

If an IRA owner is looking to buy property for the Self-Directed IRA, I recommend going through a title company to do this. There have been instances where the person selling the property is not the owner of the property. In addition, there could be liens, easements, and/or zoning violations on the property that may be undisclosed by the seller.

In the last chapter, I encouraged owners of Self-Directed IRAs to create a team of professionals to offer advice. To summarize, the owner of a Self-Directed IRA will want to avail himself or herself of their knowledge. It is important to go to a professional who knows all about the subject, rather than someone who claims to know about the subject. The cost of consulting with a professional may not be as high as is imagined.

I leave this topic with a story about another one of our clients who shared this experience. The owner of a Self-Directed IRA advised the custodian to invest $50,000.00 in an opportunity and lost the entire $50,000.00. The owner didn't want to spend the money to confer with a professional before the investment.

After the loss, this owner went to his attorney to share the story. The attorney advised this owner that he would have recommended against the investment. Interestingly enough, the consultation with the attorney cost the owner $500.00; this represents only 1.0% of the money lost in the investment.

In the next chapter, I review some of the administrative responsibilities of the IRA owner.

## HIGHLIGHTS FROM CHAPTER 4

- The owner of a Self-Directed IRA is responsible for all due diligence regarding the investments placed in the IRA.
- Individuals should take advantage of the internet's search engines to determine any information on an investment opportunity presented, including company history, company news, and company officers.
- A state's security and/or fraud division's website can contain valuable information on Ponzi schemes and fraudulent investments.
- Before investing, determine who will hold the money, if the investment is illiquid, and whether or not it is possible to lose all of the money invested.
- Be wary of investments offering steady and consistent rates of returns.
- Ponzi schemes are prevalent among affinity groups.
- An affinity group is a group of people who have an organization or community in common, such as a fraternal or business organization, a religious community, or a country club.
- There is no such thing as a "custodian-approved investment."
- An owner should check with the advisors on his/her Self-Directed IRA team before making an investment.

Chapter 4

## ADDITIONAL RESOURCES

**Sunwest Trust sponsors a channel on www.youtube.com called "sunwestira" in which many of the topics in this chapter are discussed. I recommend viewing the following to augment the information in this chapter.**

- "Self-Directed IRA Pitfalls, Risks, and Tips—Avoiding BAD Investments, Ponzi Schemes, Fraud" October 1, 2014

- "Self-Directed IRA Investing Tips-Finding the Right Information" April 28, 2015

- "Avoiding Abuses in Your IRA—Avoid Fraud in Self-Directed IRA" October 1, 2013

- "The Six Worst Things You Can Do With a Self-Directed IRA" July 16, 2013

IRA Owner's State Securities website for Fraud

Retirement Industry Trust Association
www.ritaus.org

Ponzi-Proof Your Investments: An Investor's Guide to Avoiding Ponzi Schemes and Other Fraudulent Scams
By Kathy Bazoian Phelps

# CHAPTER 5

# THE ROLE OF THE IRA OWNER IN A SELF-DIRECTED IRA—ADMINISTRATIVE RESPONSIBILITIES

In this chapter, I cover the administrative responsibilities of the IRA owner to include required minimum distributions, providing information for a required tax filing, and informing the beneficiary.

## REQUIRED MINIMUM DISTRIBUTIONS FOR A TRADITIONAL IRA

If the owner establishes the Self-Directed IRA as a Traditional IRA, SEP-IRA, or SIMPLE-IRA, the owner is responsible for implementing any required minimum distributions (RMDs).

To review, all the assets within the IRA have grown on a tax-deferred basis in a Traditional IRA; but by the time the owner attains the age of 70½, it is necessary for minimum distributions to begin so that the assets may be taxed. All of these distributions are taxable as income, except for any contributions that were made with after-tax dollars. Since Self-Directed IRAs may have illiquid assets, it is necessary for the IRA owner to plan ahead so that this does not become an issue.

I want to break down required minimum distributions a little further. According to the law that governs required minimum distributions, an IRA owner must take a minimum distribution by April 1$^{st}$ in the next year that follows the year in which the IRA owner turns age 70½. After the required minimum distributions begin, they are required to be taken by December 31$^{st}$ in every subsequent year following the year in which the IRA owner turns age 70½. This is a little confusing, so allow me to walk through two examples.

Let's assume an IRA owner turns age 70 in May 2015; the IRA owner will become 70½ in November 2015. According to the law, the IRA owner must take the minimum distribution for tax year 2015 by April 1, 2016. Since minimum distributions began in tax year 2015, the next required minimum distribution would be for tax year 2016 and this is to be taken by December 31$^{st}$, 2016. In effect, there would be two distributions in 2016, and one distribution every calendar year thereafter. Required minimum distributions are required to be taken by December 31$^{st}$.

Let's look at another example and in this one, the IRA owner turns age 70 in December 2015. This means that the IRA owner will become 70½ in June 2016. According to the law, the IRA owner must take the minimum distribution for tax year 2016 by April 1, 2017; the next required minimum distribution would be for tax year 2017 and this is to be taken by December 31$^{st}$, 2017. In effect, there would be two distributions in 2017, and one distribution every calendar year thereafter. Required minimum distributions are required to be taken by December 31$^{st}$.

An easy way to remember this is if an IRA owner turns age 70 prior to July 1$^{st}$ in the current tax year, the IRA owner has until April 1$^{st}$ in the next year to take the required minimum distribution and will also be required to take another minimum distribution by December 31$^{st}$ of that same year.

These distributions are based upon the IRA owner's life expectancy and the IRA's value on December 31$^{st}$ of the preceding year. The calculation may also take into account the IRA beneficiary's(ies') age(s). In this determination, all of the IRA owner's Traditional IRAs are aggregated to determine the IRA's total value on December 31$^{st}$ of the preceding year.

Note, a required minimum distribution does not need to be taken from every Traditional IRA. It is possible to take the entire required minimum distribution from only one of the Traditional IRAs. If the IRA owner does not make the required minimum distributions, there is a rather high penalty tax of 50% assessed on the amount which should have been distributed.

Since an IRA owner must advise the custodian to liquidate assets and issue a check for the distribution amount, it is important for the IRA owner to stay on top of the situation. I recommend the IRA owner maintain some cash in the Self-Directed IRA for distribution purposes or maintain another IRA with publicly-traded assets.

## NON-TRADITIONAL ASSET ISSUES

A characteristic of non-traditional assets is that generally they are illiquid. It is the IRA owner's responsibility to negotiate the price at which to sell the asset and to sell the asset. The custodian only advises the IRA owner that a required minimum distribution is due in the following year, and the custodian will calculate the dollar amount of the required minimum distribution, if requested to do so by the IRA owner.

The IRA owner will want to advise the custodian of what asset to sell far enough in advance so that the transaction can be completed in a timely manner to make the required minimum distribution. The IRA owner will need to be cognizant of any lead time required for the disposal of an asset.

If the Self-Directed IRA has only illiquid assets and the IRA owner does not want the custodian to sell the assets, it is possible to take a required minimum distribution of property in kind equal to the dollar amount of the required distribution. This in-kind distribution generally results in changing a portion or a percentage of the title on the asset from the custodian to the IRA owner. Keep in mind that the IRA owner may have to pay some tax on the distribution, even though it is an in-kind distribution.

For example, if the asset is real estate, a portion of the property may be transferred to the owner of the IRA and the custodian would retain the balance. The title of the property would reflect this and the custodian would report this as a dollar amount for the required minimum distribution. In order to make the in-kind distribution described, an appraisal of the property would be required and a title company should be involved.

While an in-kind distribution is possible, it may be more difficult than a cash distribution. I recommend seeking advice from an attorney, accountant, and/or tax professional in the determination of the required minimum distribution and the best course of action on which to proceed.

## PROVIDING INFORMATION FOR A REQUIRED TAX FILING

As was discussed in a previous chapter, the custodian for the Self-Directed IRA performs the record keeping for the IRA owner and is responsible for sending out the required IRS tax filings. With one of those filings, the IRA owner plays an active role in providing the information so that the custodian may complete the form on a timely basis.

IRS Form 5498 is used to report the IRA's "fair market value" (FMV) and provides the valuation of the assets held in the account as of December 31$^{st}$ of the tax year just concluded. It is required to be mailed to the IRA owner, along with a copy to the IRS, by May 31$^{st}$. It also shows any IRA contributions for the tax year just concluded and made up until April 15$^{th}$ of the current year, and any cash that is held in the account. This form is for information purposes only and is not needed for income-tax filing.

The IRS Form 5498 identifies the type of IRA held, for example Traditional, Roth, SEP, or SIMPLE; and IRA contributions, as well as any Roth IRA conversion amounts. In addition, if a required minimum distribution is to be made in the following year, the date on which the owner attains age 70½ is shown. The IRS requires custodians to provide the fair market value for each account annually, and a separate Form 5498 is required for each type of IRA owned by an individual.

For tax years 2015 and later, the IRS is requesting the market value and identification of specific assets which are pertinent to Self-Directed IRAs.

The following categories of assets are listed: stock or other ownership interest in a corporation that is not readily tradeable on an established securities market; short-or long-term debt obligation that is not traded on an established securities market; ownership interest in a limited liability company or similar entity (unless the interest is publicly traded on an established securities market); real estate; ownership interest in a partnership, trust, or similar entity (unless the interest is publicly traded on an established securities market); option contract or similar contract that is not offered for trade on an established option exchange; and any other asset that does not have a readily available fair market value.

Self-Directed IRAs hold a wide variety of assets from private companies, to gold, to real estate located all over the country; and this is where the IRA owner comes in, since the custodian cannot be expected to accurately value those types of assets. It is the IRA owner who provides the value of the non-traditional assets that do not have a published market value, and the IRA owner will generally receive a request from the custodian for this to be done. I recommend an IRA owner work with a third party so that the valuations of the assets are at arm's length and truly fair.

If the IRA owner has a piece of real estate or a private company, it is a good idea for the owner to hire an independent third party to provide a valuation. In my opinion, an IRA owner with real estate does not have to get a full-blown appraisal in order to come up with a value of a property. If the IRA owner has a friend or close associate who is a realtor, the owner could ask the realtor to run some "comps" of homes or apartments (or whatever the property type happens to be) in the location of the property. In this way, the realtor could use market information to come up with a decent estimate for the value of the property; and it should be determined as fair, since the realtor is not related to the IRA owner.

If an IRA owner has gold in the account, the market value could be obtained by multiplying the spot price of gold by the number of ounces held in the account. Note, if the IRA owner has a limited liability company, all the assets within the limited liability company will need to be valued. If there is debt or a promissory note, that asset will need to be valued, as well.

**INFORMING THE BENEFICIARY**

One of the great things about Self-Directed IRAs is that an owner can have many different types of investments; but how can an owner make sure that loved ones stay informed? It is important to let the beneficiaries on Self-Directed IRAs know the type of assets they will inherit and have responsibility for managing, as well as the rules pertaining to those assets.

The hands-on effort required in managing a Self-Directed IRA is something to keep in mind when naming a beneficiary(ies). While the owner of the IRA may have a high level of experience or expertise in the assets within the Self-Directed IRA, the beneficiary(ies) may have little or no experience; this could present issues for the beneficiary. I believe it is the owner's responsibility to think ahead for the beneficiary's(ies') sake.

Let's take a moment to review the rules relating to inherited IRAs.

**INHERITED SELF-DIRECTED IRA ESTABLISHED AS A TRADITIONAL IRA**

If the Self-Directed IRA is established as a Traditional IRA, and only the spouse is named to receive benefits, the spouse can either assume ownership of that account; "roll" (move) that account into his/her own IRA; or may continue to remain as beneficiary.

Any IRA that is continued by the beneficiary (excluding the spouse of the deceased owner) is retitled as an inherited IRA, for example, "Sunwest Trust Custodian for Jane Adams Brown, beneficiary of John Adams Inherited IRA."

If the spouse assumes ownership, then his/her age is used to determine the start of required minimum distributions. When the spouse remains as beneficiary of the Traditional IRA, required minimum distributions on the account begin in the year the deceased IRA owner would have become age 70½. If the IRA owner dies at age 70½ or later after required minimum distributions have started, distributions continue.

If another individual(s) or entity(ies) is named beneficiary(ies), then a set of required minimum distribution rules apply in the year following the deceased IRA owner's death, ranging from using the IRA owner's age, the beneficiary's(ies') age(s), and/or alternately a five-year payout. All distributions are income taxable when received; however, any contributions that were made with after-tax dollars are received income-tax free.

## INHERITED SELF-DIRECTED IRA ESTABLISHED AS A ROTH IRA

If the Self-Directed IRA was established as a Roth IRA, required minimum distribution rules are applied after the IRA owner's death to the Roth assets held by the beneficiary(ies). **While there are no required minimum distribution rules associated with a Roth IRA while the IRA owner is alive, in effect, the assets of a Roth IRA are required to be distributed after the IRA owner's death.**

73

The distribution begins in the year following the deceased IRA owner's death; and the option for the distribution of these assets is either a lump sum, a five-year payout, or over the lifetime of the beneficiary.

Any IRA that is continued by the beneficiary (excluding the spouse of the deceased owner) is retitled as an inherited IRA, for example, "Sunwest Trust Custodian for Jane Adams Brown, beneficiary of John Adams Inherited IRA."

If only the spouse is named to receive benefits, the surviving spouse has more latitude. The spouse can either assume ownership of that account; "roll" (move) that account into his/her own Roth IRA; or may continue to remain as beneficiary.

In situations where the spouse remains as beneficiary of the Roth IRA and the IRA owner died before age 70½, the spouse isn't required to begin distributions in the year following the deceased IRA owner's death; but may begin the required minimum distributions on the account in the year the deceased IRA owner would have become age 70½.

If another individual(s) or entity is named beneficiary(ies), then a set of required minimum distribution rules apply ranging from using the IRA owner's age and/or the beneficiary's(ies') age(s), and/or a mandatory five-year payout. All distributions from the Roth IRA are income-tax free, if the account had been established for five years.

## A FINAL NOTE ON RMDs

In all instances regarding required-minimum-distribution scenarios upon the death of the IRA owner irrespective of whether it is a Traditional IRA or a Roth IRA, if the required minimum distribution is not taken, then the 50% penalty tax applies to the amount that should have been distributed.

## BENEFICIARY MANAGEMENT ISSUES

It is a difficult time when a loved one dies, and the last thing the IRA owner would want to do is make it more difficult for the loved one(s) named as beneficiary(ies). Upon the death of an IRA owner, the first thing a beneficiary(ies) will need to do is provide a death certificate to the custodian of the Self-Directed IRA to change the account registration to an inherited IRA (except in those instances when a spouse inherits). I recommend that the beneficiary(ies) talk with the attorney, accountant, or tax professional to discuss the beneficiary options, plan a course of action, and review the IRA assets.

Will the IRA assets need to be liquidated? Do the assets generate income? The assets may not be marketable or easy to liquidate, and the beneficiary(ies) will want to have professional help to understand the inherited IRA account options, and assets.

Here is a case in point. Upon the passing of one of our Self-Directed IRA clients, the beneficiary called our office. The beneficiary had not been informed of the nature of the assets, how to proceed, or what to expect when the IRA was inherited. As a result, the beneficiary called wanting to know what a limited liability company (LLC) was and if our office had any information regarding the nature of the LLC that was in the inherited IRA.

Unfortunately for her, IRA custodians cannot help much with LLC investments, so she had to determine the nature of the LLC's assets on her own. If her spouse had let her know the nature of the IRA-LLC assets to be inherited, it may have given her some direction in which to proceed, rather than starting at ground zero with no information.

Based upon this instance, our company developed the *Self-Directed IRA Beneficiaries' Information Form*. This form tells beneficiaries some of what they need to know about inherited Self-Directed IRAs, with whom the beneficiary(ies) needs to work, what the beneficiary(ies) needs to do with the assets, and whom to call for assistance.

By using this form, an IRA owner can save loved ones lots of time and energy by giving them all the inherited IRA information that is needed for the illiquid and/or specialized investments that may be in the account. An IRA owner is able to share with the beneficiary(ies) the contact information of anyone from whom investments were purchased, and the contact information of trusted advisors who may be able to help the beneficiary(ies).

Although our company created the form our clients use, any owner of a Self-Directed IRA can create a form to use, since it is only for the owner's personal use. After authorizing a custodian to hold this information, it is kept safe until it is needed by the beneficiary(ies). At that time, the custodian is authorized to release the information to the beneficiary(ies). I recommend reviewing and updating this information every year, especially if changes are made to investments. By informing beneficiaries of the assets to be inherited, they will be ready when an unplanned event happens; and things will be easier for loved ones.

In the next chapter, the role of the owner in determining prohibited transactions is discussed in detail.

## HIGHLIGHTS FROM CHAPTER 5

- **Due to the nature of illiquid assets within a Self-Directed IRA, the owner of a Traditional IRA needs to plan ahead for required minimum distributions (RMDs).**
- **It is the IRA owner's responsibility to negotiate the price at which to sell the asset and to sell the asset, in order to meet the required minimum distribution deadline.**
- **It is the owner's responsibility to provide the custodian the fair market value of non-traditional assets that do not have a market value, so that the custodian can prepare IRS Form 5498 on a timely basis.**
- **The hands-on effort required in managing a Self-Directed IRA is something to keep in mind when naming a beneficiary.**
- **An owner can provide critical information to the beneficiary by outlining what they need to know about inherited Self-Directed IRAs, with whom the beneficiary needs to work, what the beneficiary needs to do with the assets, and whom to call for assistance.**

## ADDITIONAL RESOURCES

**Sunwest Trust sponsors a channel on www.youtube.com called "sunwestira" in which many of the topics in this chapter are discussed. I recommend viewing the following to augment the information in this chapter.**

- "IRA End of Year Deadlines" December 16, 2014

- "What is the Fair Market Value of my IRA?" December 9, 2014

- "How to Conduct a Fair Market Evaluation for Self-Directed IRA" December 7, 2015

- "IRA Tax Documents Form 5498" March 17, 2015

- "What is a Form 5498 and Form 5498 Changes" January 17, 2015

- "Required Minimum Distribution Rules—What You Need to Know" December 2, 2014

- "Choosing a Beneficiary" February 17, 2015

- "Self-Directed IRA Beneficiary Guidelines" January 27, 2015

- "Self-Directed IRA Beneficiary Information" February 24, 2015

- "Inherited IRA Rules for a Self-Directed IRA" February 3, 2015

# CHAPTER 6

# PROHIBITED TRANSACTIONS

I touched briefly on prohibited transactions in Chapter 3 as the subject related to reviewing a Self-Directed IRA plan document. Note that prohibited transactions apply to IRAs with traditional assets and all qualified retirement plans, as well.

> **In effect, a prohibited transaction is not a type of property or asset. A prohibited transaction is the improper use of the IRA by the owner, the beneficiary, or a disqualified person.**

The probability of an IRA with traditional assets engaging in a prohibited transaction with a disqualified person may not be as high as with a Self-Directed IRA with non-traditional assets however, since traditional investments generally are in large, publicly-traded stocks, and/or in bank CDs, mutual funds, or annuities. Generally, the IRA is purchasing or selling traditional investments from large financial institutions or mutual fund families. Family members or family-owned businesses are not involved in those transactions.

Prohibited transaction information is found in Internal Revenue Code Section 4975, and it is indeed complex. It is one of the reasons that I recommend establishing a team of professionals before setting up a Self-Directed IRA and consulting with this team of professionals before directing the custodian to make a purchase on behalf of the Self-Directed IRA.

## PROHIBITED TRANSACTIONS DEFINED

To restate, a prohibited transaction is the improper use of the IRA by the owner, the beneficiary, or a disqualified person. Disqualified persons are a class of people who include the fiduciary, the owner's spouse, ancestors, lineal descendants, and their spouses.

According to IRC Section 4975(c)(1), the general rule for prohibited transactions includes:

- any direct or indirect sale or exchange, or leasing, of any property between an IRA and a disqualified person;
- the lending of money or other extension of credit between an IRA and a disqualified person;
- the furnishing of goods, services, or facilities between an IRA and a disqualified person;
- the transfer to, or use by or for the benefit of, a disqualified person of the income or assets of an IRA;
- the act by a disqualified person who is a fiduciary whereby he deals with the income or assets of the IRA in his own interests or for his own account; or
- the receipt of any consideration for his own personal account by any disqualified person who is a fiduciary from any party dealing with the IRA in connection with a transaction involving the income or assets of the IRA.

## DISQUALIFIED PERSONS IDENTIFIED

The owner of a Self-Directed IRA is the one making the decisions on the investments, and the IRA owner may be the one most likely to engage in a prohibited transaction with the IRA, either directly or indirectly. It is important that the IRA owner identify other disqualified persons who may be associated with each transaction.

In addition to the IRA owner, a disqualified person is the owner's spouse; the owner's ancestors to include, mother and father, grandmother and grandfather, and great grandmother and great grandfather, etc.; and the owner's lineal descendants to include the owner's children and their spouses, grandchildren and their spouses, and great grand-children and their spouses, etc.

A disqualified person is also any entity(ies) in which the IRA owner or disqualified person(s) owns a 50% or more interest; an officer, director, a 10% or more shareholder or a highly compensated employee of the IRA owner, disqual-ified person(s) or an entity(ies) in which the IRA owner or disqualified person(s) owns a 50% or more interest.

A disqualified person also includes the fiduciary on the account and the beneficiary on the IRA.

I recommend a Self-Directed IRA owner become totally familiar with those persons and/or entities identified as a disqualified person in order to avoid issues.

## IMPACT OF A PROHIBITED TRANSACTION BY THE IRA OWNER OR BENEFICIARY

The impact of a prohibited transaction to an IRA is major. If an IRA owner or beneficiary engages in a prohibited transaction, the IRA is disqualified and loses its favorable tax status as of January 1 of the tax year in which the prohibited transaction occurred. The assets of the IRA are distributed as of the prohibited transaction date; the fair market value of the assets as of the January 1 date of the year in which the prohibited transaction occurred is used.

## TRADITIONAL IRAs

For a Traditional IRA or SEP-IRA, if the IRA owner is below age 59½, the entire distribution is taxable as personal income in the year the prohibited transaction occurred. In addition, there is a 10% excise penalty on the assets distributed as income, because it is considered a premature distribution.

If the account is a SIMPLE-IRA and the IRA owner is below age 59½, the entire distribution is taxable as personal income in the year the prohibited transaction occurred; and there is a 25% excise penalty on the premature distribution.

If the IRA owner is age 59½ or above, neither the 10% excise penalty for an IRA or SEP-IRA, nor the 25% penalty for the SIMPLE-IRA applies. Note that the entire distribution is still taxable as personal income in the year the prohibited transaction occurred.

In all of the foregoing instances, if any of the contributions made to the Traditional IRA, SEP-IRA, or SIMPLE-IRA were made with after-tax dollars, these contributions are distributed income-tax free.

## ROTH IRAs

For a Roth IRA, if the owner is below age 59½ the part of the distribution representing the untaxed growth on any investment gains or income is taxable as personal income in the year the prohibited transaction occurred, since it is not a qualified distribution. Further, the income is subject to the 10% excise penalty, since the owner is below age 59½. If there are conversion amounts in the account that have not been in the IRA for five years, those amounts are subject to the 10% excise penalty, as well.

If the Roth IRA owner is age 59½ or above and the account has been established for five years, the distribution as a result of a prohibited transaction would be treated as a qualified distribution and not taxable.

## POSSIBLE EXCEPTION

Note, in all instances, there may be the possibility that the 10% excise penalty for distributions below age 59½ would not apply to a prohibited-transaction distribution, if the distribution also met one of the exceptions to the premature distribution rule (disability, for example).

## DISQUALIFICATION IMPACT

With the disqualification of the IRA, any transactions that took place within the Traditional IRA, SEP-IRA, SIMPLE-IRA, or Roth IRA, from the time that the prohibited transaction occurred, will now have to be treated as transactions that did not take place within a tax-sheltered or tax-free environment. These transactions will be treated as the IRA owner's personal transactions and will be subject to taxation. Depending on the date the prohibited transaction occurred and the date on which it was discovered, the IRA owner may have to file amended returns.

This aspect may be a little easier to understand with an example. Let's say a prohibited transaction took place in tax year 2012, but was not discovered until tax year 2014. In this scenario, any transactions that occurred within the IRA between January 1, 2012, and the date on which the prohibited transaction was discovered and reported, could be subject to taxation either as ordinary income or capital gains. This is due to the fact the IRA status was disallowed effective January 1, 2012. This could necessitate the IRA owner having to file an amended return for tax years 2012 and 2013; there may be additional tax due, and tax penalties, as well.

Needless to say, an IRA owner will want to avoid prohibited transactions due to the potentially severe ramifications.

## IMPACT OF A PROHIBITED TRANSACTION BY SOMEONE OTHER THAN THE IRA OWNER OR BENEFICIARY

If a prohibited transaction occurs between the IRA and a disqualified person other than the IRA owner or beneficiary, there is an excise tax of 15% of the value of the transaction imposed on the individual(s) or entity(ies) who engaged in the transaction. If the transaction is not corrected within a certain period of time, the excise penalty increases to 100% of the value of the transaction.

As I mentioned previously, it may be easier for an owner of a Self-Directed IRA to run afoul of a prohibited transaction due to the nature of non-traditional assets and the fact that it is generally the IRA owner who is making the investment decisions. The following section outlines some scenarios depicting prohibited transactions.

## EXAMPLES OF BUYING, SELLING, LENDING, LEASING TRANSACTIONS WITH DISQUALIFIED PERSONS

An IRA owner or disqualified person is not allowed to sell property or assets to the IRA. This includes stock that he/she may own, a rental property, an option to buy the property, etc. The IRA must purchase the property from a disinterested third party.

Let's say an IRA owner owns a rental property outside of the IRA that is a good, income-producing asset and he/she wants to sell it to the IRA. This is not possible without creating a prohibited transaction since the IRA owner is a disqualified person and may not sell property to the IRA. If, on the other hand, the IRA owner's brother owns the rental property, the IRA could purchase it from the brother, since siblings of the owner are not disqualified persons.

Let's assume, the rental property in the last scenario was owned by the IRA owner's brother and the IRA purchased the property and now owns it. The IRA owner wants to allow his widowed mother to live in this property. This is not possible without creating a prohibited transaction, since the IRA owner's mother is a disqualified person and a disqualified person may not lease property from an IRA or use the property for personal benefit. Although the owner's mother may not live in the house, the owner can lease the house to a disinterested third party.

In another example, the tenants in a rental property owned by the IRA call the IRA owner informing him/her of a repair issue. The IRA owner is quite handy with tools and decides to make the repairs himself/herself. This is not a good idea, since this could be a situation of a disqualified person providing services and creating a prohibited transaction. In this instance, the IRA owner should call a disinterested third party to make the repairs.

For a final scenario, the IRA owner's son-in-law is an employee at a tech company and has been given stock options; the IRA owner instructs the custodian to buy the stock options from his son-in-law so that the IRA may purchase the stock. This could be a prohibited transaction since the son-in-law who owns the options is a disqualified person. If the son-on-law has a co-worker at the company who is willing to sell the options, the IRA could purchase the options from the co-worker.

## EXAMPLES OF LOANS AND SECURING DEBT

The IRA owner is not allowed to secure the debt of an IRA or use the IRA as collateral for a personal loan. Debt issues may come into play if the IRA wants to purchase real estate.

Generally speaking, the IRA should have enough in the account to purchase the property out right or may be able to obtain seller financing after a down payment. The IRA owner may not sign a promissory note to guarantee the loan, nor may the owner pledge any assets that are personally owned to guarantee the loan, since this could be a prohibited transaction. This holds true for any of the disqualified persons (entities) previously listed, as well.

In the above instance, if there is no seller financing available, the IRA may be able to obtain a non-recourse loan. A non-recourse loan is one in which the asset is the only item that secures the loan; the lender cannot go after the IRA's assets, nor can the lender go after the assets of the IRA owner. Banks that specialize in non-recourse loans for Self-Directed IRAs may be found by doing a search on the internet.

In another example, an IRA owner's son actively buys houses, fixes them up, and then rents them. The son approaches the IRA owner to request a loan from the IRA and offers to pay a market interest rate on the borrowed funds. If the IRA makes a loan to the IRA owner's son, this could be a prohibited transaction since the son is a disqualified person. The son then approaches his uncle who also owns a Self-Directed IRA, and the IRA loans the nephew the money at the market interest rate. This is not a prohibited transaction since a nephew is not a disqualified person.

Let's say the IRA owner's daughter and the daughter's business partner own a catering business in which the daughter's ownership share is 45%. The catering business has requested a loan from the IRA at a market interest rate, and the IRA owner has instructed the custodian to loan the business the money. This is not a prohibited transaction since the daughter's interest is less than 50% and the business which is borrowing the money is not a disqualified person. If, on the other hand, the daughter owned the 55% share of the business, it could be a prohibited transaction. The business could be a disqualified person since the daughter's share was 50% or greater.

Under another scenario, an IRA owner wants to buy commodities on margin for his/her Self-Directed IRA. This means that borrowed money is used to purchase the commodities. Upon a review of the margin agreement, it is disclosed that the investor could lose all of the money invested and it is possible to lose more than the money invested. By signing the margin agreement, the IRA owner agrees to make up the difference if more money than what is invested is lost in the transactions. It is the IRA custodian's position that the owner would be securing the debt of the IRA and this could be a prohibited transaction.

## EXAMPLES IN SELF-DEALING TRANSACTIONS

This area of the law has to do with the IRA owner or any other disqualified person(s) or entity(ies) obtaining benefit from a transaction with the IRA.

Let's take an example of a Self-Directed IRA owned by a realtor. The owner desires the IRA to invest in rental property and finds the perfect house for the IRA to purchase. Generally, there is a commission involved in the sale of real estate; and if the realtor who is the buyer's agent and is also the IRA owner and a disqualified person, receives this commission on the sale, it could be an example of self-dealing. This could result in a prohibited transaction. The realtor will probably need to forego the commission on the house in order to avoid a prohibited transaction.

This next example comes from one of our clients. Our client owned a Self-Directed IRA in which there was a substantial cash position. In addition, and outside of the IRA structure, this client personally owned an LLC. The LLC owned a piece of property that it intended to sell to a non-disqualified party. The owner of the Self-Directed IRA planned to offer a private mortgage to the buyer of the home through his Self-Directed IRA and asked for the custodian's opinion on the transaction.

As I do with all the inquiries we receive, I advised him to talk to his tax professional, since custodians do not give legal, accounting, or tax advice. Further, it would be his tax professional who would represent him if anything went awry. I also advised him to determine if the mortgage he was proposing was consistent with mortgage rules for Self-Directed IRAs.

I suggested that he may want to determine if the borrower could qualify for a mortgage loan elsewhere. If the borrower could not qualify for a mortgage elsewhere, and the Self-Directed IRA loaned the purchaser of the property the amount for the mortgage, it could be viewed that the IRA owner would benefit from this transaction, since he personally owned the LLC that was selling the property.

In effect, although the LLC with the property for sale was owned personally outside of the IRA, it is the IRA owner who could benefit by offering the mortgage, if the purchaser was unable to qualify for a mortgage elsewhere. The personally-owned LLC would only be able to sell the property, because of the IRA owner's Self-Directed IRA being able to make a loan to the purchaser. If that were the case, it was my opinion that the private mortgage may be an example of self-dealing, and consequently could be a prohibited transaction.

On the other hand, if the purchaser of the property could qualify for a mortgage elsewhere, the selling of the property and the offering of the mortgage are not tied together. The mortgage offered by the Self-Directed IRA at a market rate could just be viewed as a good investment.

Unlike the examples of buying, selling, lending, leasing, and loans and securing debt, the self-dealing transactions may be a little more difficult to recognize. Tax Court and Department of Labor rulings regarding this concept have been inconsistent in this area of the law. This is where a team of professionals will serve the IRA owner well.

## SUMMARY

Regarding prohibited transactions, knowledge is power. I recommend that any individual wishing to establish a Self-Directed IRA avail himself/herself of a team of professionals to act as a guide in navigating these issues.

It's not difficult to avoid prohibited transactions; the IRA owner should simply avoid transactions with disqualified persons. It is my opinion that individuals get themselves into trouble when they try to circumvent the regulations of the

Internal Revenue Code.


In the next two chapters, I cover some popular investment ideas for Self-Directed IRAs.

## HIGHLIGHTS FROM CHAPTER 6

- A prohibited transaction is the improper use of the IRA by the owner, the beneficiary, or a disqualified person.
- Disqualified persons are a class of people who include the fiduciary, the owner's spouse, ancestors, lineal descendants, and their spouses.
- An IRA owner, beneficiary, or disqualified person is not allowed to sell, lease, exchange, or lend property to the IRA.
- An IRA owner, beneficiary, or disqualified person is not allowed to secure the debt of an IRA or use the IRA for collateral.
- An IRA owner, beneficiary, or disqualified person may not obtain a benefit from an IRA. This is known as self-dealing.
- If an IRA owner or beneficiary engages in a prohibited transaction, the IRA is disqualified and loses its favorable tax status as of January 1 of the tax year in which the prohibited transaction occurred.
- The assets of the IRA are distributed as of the prohibited transaction date and using the fair market value as of January 1 of the tax year in which the prohibited transaction occurred.
- If the owner is below age 59½ and the IRA is a Traditional IRA, SEP-IRA, or SIMPLE IRA, the entire distribution is taxable as personal income in the year the prohibited transaction occurred. (Contributions made with after-tax dollars are not treated as income.)
- For Traditional IRAs and SEP-IRAs, there is a

10% excise penalty on the assets distributed as personal income if the owner is below age 59½.

- For SIMPLE-IRAs, there is a 25% excise penalty on the assets distributed as personal income if the owner is below age 59½

- For a Roth IRA, if the owner is below age 59½ the part of the distribution representing the untaxed growth on any investment gains or income is taxable as personal income in the year the prohibited transaction occurred.

- The personal income distributed from a Roth IRA is subject to the 10% excise penalty, since the owner is below age 59½.

- Any conversion amounts in the account that have not been in the Roth IRA for five years are subject to the 10% excise penalty, as well, since the Roth IRA owner is below age 59½.

- If the Roth IRA owner is age 59½ or above and the account has been established for five years, the distribution as a result of a prohibited transaction would be treated as a qualified distribution and not taxable.

- After a prohibited transaction and disqualification of the IRA, any transactions that occurred from the date of the prohibited transaction and the date when it was discovered, are treated as the personal transactions of the owner and are taxable.

Chapter 6

## ADDITIONAL RESOURCES

Sunwest Trust sponsors a channel on www.youtube.com called "sunwestira" in which many of the topics in this chapter are discussed. I recommend viewing the following to augment the information in this chapter.

- "The Six Worst Things You Can Do With a Self-Directed IRA" July 16, 2013

- "Peek v. Commissioner: How to Avoid Costly Prohibited Transactions in a Self-Directed IRA" July 2, 2013

- "Example of a Non-Recourse Loan Investment in my Roth IRA" January 14, 2014

- "Using IRA as Collateral for Loan to Buy Rental Property: Is it possible?" June 10, 2014

- "Buying Commodities, Futures, and Options on Margin in a Self-Directed IRA-IRC Section 4975" September 3, 2015

- "What Can a Self-Directed IRA Invest In? Buying Private Stock in a Company I Work For" October 13, 2015

- "Can a Self-Directed IRA-LLC That Owns a Property Hold the Mortgage for a Non-Qualified Third Party?" October 18, 2015

- "Can I Transfer or Contribute Personal or Family Member's Investment Property to a Self-Directed Roth?" November 20, 2015

IRC Section 4975

IRS Publication 590-B

The Self-Directed IRA Handbook
by Mat Sorensen, Attorney at Law

"The Do's and Don'ts of Self Directed Investing with Retirement Accounts"
by Tom W. Anderson and The Retirement Industry Trust Association
http://www.ritaus.org/assets/documents/RITA.Prohibited.T ransactionsforinvestors.final.12.15.10.pdf

# CHAPTER 7

# SOME TYPES OF NON-TRADITIONAL ASSETS FOR A SELF-DIRECTED IRA— EQUITY-BASED AND OTHER

The book thus far has given an overview of the Self-Directed IRA from the point of view of the knowledge and time required by the owner, and has contrasted a Self-Directed IRA with non-traditional assets with that of an IRA with traditional assets.

Now, I will describe some of the more popular assets that may be placed in a Self-Directed IRA. As may be recalled, the only assets that are prohibited in a Self-Directed IRA are collectibles, life insurance, and Sub-Chapter S corporations. This leaves the investment field for Self-Directed IRAs wide open, limited only by what the custodian of the Self-Directed IRA will hold, and by what is not a prohibited transaction or a transaction with a disqualified person/entity.

In this chapter, I'll discuss equity-based investments and precious metals. In the next chapter, I'll focus on debt-based investments. Before investing, I recommend the owner of a Self-Directed IRA review any investments with his/her team of professionals.

I'll begin by describing a Self-Directed IRA Single Member Limited Liability Company (IRA-LLC) which can actually give the owner checkbook control over some of the IRA assets.

## THE IRA SINGLE MEMBER LIMITED LIABILITY COMPANY (IRA-LLC)

A Limited Liability Company is a business structure composed of members, and generally one in which the members are not held personally liable for the company's debts or liabilities. Any income generated by the LLC flows through to the member. LLCs are popular for the ease in which one can be established. In effect, the LLC issues membership units and an individual may purchase these units much in the same way mutual fund shares or stocks are purchased.

Generally speaking, in a Self-Directed IRA, the IRA establishes and funds a single member LLC; it is 100% owned by the Self-Directed IRA; and it is held by the custodian as an asset of the Self-Directed IRA. The IRA owner can serve as the non-compensated manager of the LLC and as such, is able to enter into contracts on behalf of the LLC, make investment decisions, and write checks upon the LLC's checking account. With an IRA-LLC, the liability stops with the LLC; neither the assets of the IRA, the IRA owner, nor the IRA custodian may be attached to satisfy the liabilities of the IRA-LLC.

The IRA-LLC manager and/or the IRA owner (if different from the manager) must be careful not to personally guarantee any of the debt or obligations of the IRA-LLC. For this reason, it is wise to have an attorney review any documents to be signed by the IRA owner in his/her capacity as the IRA-LLC manager.

The membership of the LLC is in the name of the custodian for the benefit of the IRA owner, for example, "Sunwest Trust Custodian for John Adams Self-Directed IRA." It is noted that the name of the LLC may be any name the IRA owner desires.

I caution individuals before setting up an IRA-LLC to determine that the custodian of their Self-Directed IRA will allow an IRA-LLC to be held as an asset. Further, after determining whether the custodian will hold the IRA-LLC as an asset, it is necessary to determine if the custodian will permit the IRA to be the non-compensated manager of the IRA-LLC. Not all custodians who hold non-traditional assets will permit the IRA-LLC structure.

As with the Self-Directed IRA, the IRA owner should have some idea of the type of assets the IRA-LLC will acquire, and in what state those assets will be acquired. Purchasing assets in various states may require the IRA-LLC to be registered in that particular state. If foreign property (outside the United States) is purchased, it is the IRA-LLC manager's/IRA owner's responsibility to know the necessary requirements. It is necessary to check the specifics in the area/state/country in which the IRA-LLC is purchasing the assets.

If the owner of a Self-Directed IRA desires to establish an IRA-LLC, I recommend that the owner contact an attorney who is knowledgeable regarding Self-Directed IRAs to create the documents necessary for the LLC. The LLC documents include articles of organization and the operating agreement.

The operating agreement may state the number of units in which the IRA is investing and the amount being invested. In addition, the operating agreement should state that the IRA-LLC's manager is not to be compensated and should limit the IRA-LLC manager's activities to administrative activities. I recommend IRA owners conduct their due diligence in this regard, as the cost for establishing an IRA-LLC varies widely.

The IRA-LLC manager is not to provide any kind of services to the LLC; otherwise, the IRA-LLC manager who is the generally the IRA owner and is also a disqualified person, could be engaging in a prohibited transaction. A tax identification number for the IRA-LLC must be obtained by the IRA-LLC manager. Note that the IRA owner may not transfer an already existing LLC that the IRA owner has created into the IRA; this could be a prohibited transaction.

The IRA-LLC operating agreement is delivered to the custodian of the Self-Directed IRA for review and as evidence of the asset; the custodian signs the operating agreement on behalf of the IRA, for example, "Sunwest Trust Custodian for John Adams Self-Directed IRA." The IRA owner then completes a Direction of Investment form for the amount of money needed to purchase the membership units of the IRA-LLC.

The custodian may make the check payable to the IRA-LLC, and the IRA-LLC manager deposits the check into the checking account that is set up for the IRA-LLC. Alternatively, the custodian may wire the funds directly to the bank in which the IRA-LLC's checking account is established.

If and when the IRA-LLC requires additional funding, the owner of the Self-Directed IRA completes a Direction of

Investment form, directing the custodian to purchase additional membership units. Alternatively, the IRA-LLC may require a "capital call," wherein the actual number of membership units does not increase, but rather the dollar value of the units outstanding increases.

Even though the IRA owner is the manager of the IRA-LLC and can actively write checks to purchase investments (ultimately bypassing the custodian), the owner must still abide by the prohibited transaction rules, and must be cognizant of engaging the IRA-LLC in any prohibited transaction with a disqualified person. It is noted the IRA-LLC is used in most cases for its convenience.

Recordkeeping is an extremely important activity for the IRA-LLC manager. The IRA-LLC manager is required to keep track of all investments and expenses, to record income from the assets, and to write checks. In addition, the IRA-LLC manager has the responsibility of providing the asset valuation information as of December 31st to the custodian, since the IRA-LLC is part of the Self-Directed IRA assets.

I want to add a final word regarding the IRA-LLC manager's check-writing ability. The manager of an IRA-LLC may not write a check that is a distribution to the IRA owner. Any distributions from the Self-Directed IRA must be made by the custodian.

## THINKING OUTSIDE THE BOX WITH AN IRA-LLC

I want to share a story about one of our clients who lives in the Midwest. This client had a Self-Directed IRA and wanted to establish an LLC in his IRA. When he was asked in what the IRA-LLC would invest, he answered "cows," and proceeded to explain his plan.

This client had been going to cattle auctions, buying cows, and then selling them to other ranchers for a profit. He had years of experience in doing this. His thought was to move this type of business to his IRA-LLC.

His IRA-LLC would hire one of his friends who is a non-disqualified person to go to the auction to purchase the cows on behalf of the IRA-LLC. The IRA-LLC would then sell the cows to the other ranchers for a profit, and the sales proceeds would go back into the IRA-LLC. The plan appeared solid, and this was an industry in which the IRA owner was familiar.

Note that the IRS may consider this a "business," and the Unrelated Business Income Tax (UBIT) may be triggered. I recommend the IRA owner consult with the tax professional on his/her team of professionals, before the IRA-LLC engages in business activities.

## PRIVATE OFFERINGS

Owners of Self-Directed IRAs may be made aware of investment opportunities in private offerings, and by that I mean non-public offerings. That is one of the things that makes owning a Self-Directed IRA attractive. In this respect, whether the Self-Directed IRA purchases shares or units in an offering, I recommend the owner become familiar with the different types of business entities which are making the private offering, and the risk to personal assets that may be involved with the different type of business entities.

To review, a Self-Directed IRA may not invest in a Sub-Chapter S corporation, but it may invest in any other type of business entity. Let's take a look at the different business entities or opportunities.

## General Partnership

A general partnership is a business structure in which all partners work for the benefit of the partnership and handle the day-to-day activities of the partnership. There is no separate tax bracket for the partnership; the income, tax benefits, and capital gains are passed through to the partners as individuals.

Each partner shares in the income of the partnership according to one's partnership share or interest in the partnership. In addition, each partner is responsible for the debts and liabilities of the partnership. In this arrangement, creditors may go after the personal assets of all the partners, which may include the Self-Directed IRA.

## Limited Partnership

A limited partnership is often used as a means of raising capital. It has one general partner who is responsible for the day-to-day decision making and business activities. The limited partners generally contribute capital to the partnership; they are not responsible for the day-to-day activities or the day-to-day business decisions.

There is no separate tax bracket for the limited partnership; the income, tax benefits, and capital gains are passed through to the partners as individuals, according to their share. Unlike the general partnership, the limited partner's liability is limited to one's investment in the limited partnership, and no more.

## Limited Liability Company

A limited liability company (LLC) is a business structure composed of members, and generally one in which the members are not held personally liable for the company's debts or liabilities. Any income generated by the LLC flows through to the members as individuals. LLCs are popular for the ease with which they can be established. In effect, the LLC issues membership units and an individual may purchase these units.

## C Corporation

The C Corporation is a business entity that has shareholders whose interest is represented by shares or ownership percentages in the business. The C Corporation has its own tax bracket. Any profit is taxed at the corporate level; dividends are paid to the shareholders of the corporation in proportion to their ownership interest. The owners and shareholders of the C Corporation are not held liable for the company's debts or obligations.

## Private Placement

A private placement or offering occurs when a company sells its securities to raise money in a non-public offering. Generally speaking, the companies are too small to be on the public market. In this respect, there may be limited financial information on the company, as well as limited information on the issuer and/or the management.

The money invested may be tied up for a long time, since the issuer of the securities does not have to provide liquidity to the investors. Although often offered to accredited investors who meet income and net worth requirements, and who may be able to withstand a total loss of the investment; a private placement offering may be made to non-accredited investors, as well.

## Joint Venture

Joint Ventures are single business transactions formed for a limited period of time to accomplish a goal or a common project. Investors put up money for the project, and generally an expert in the field or industry of the joint venture provides the expertise for the investment. Joint ventures are usually set up between two or more individuals where investors share in relationship to their participation in the joint venture.

Business Start-Ups

It is possible that the Self-Directed IRA may want to invest in local or regional business enterprises. One of our clients wanted to invest some of his Self-Directed IRA money in his neighbor's start-up business; the business offers beef jerky. Some start-up opportunities may be found through business-incubator organizations. These incubator organizations help develop start-up or new businesses in management, marketing, and financial operations.

In addition, the owner of a Self-Directed IRA may find it beneficial to join a regional angel network to identify potential investment opportunities. Another of our clients joined a regional network that follows the guidelines and procedures of the national angel network, and is investing in technology and healthcare start-ups and new businesses. I recommend the owner of a Self-Directed IRA review any investments with his/her team of professionals to determine that the investment is in line with retirement goals and does not constitute a prohibited transaction or a transaction with a disqualified person.

## CROWDFUNDING

The Securities and Exchange Commission (SEC) adopted Regulation Crowdfunding as announced in their press release dated October 30, 2015. The final rules were published for comment and will be adopted into law after a period of time for comments, and the consideration of those comments.

Crowdfunding appears in Title III of the Jumpstart Our Business Startups Act (JOBS ACT) that was enacted April 5, 2012. This is a way for businesses that are looking for capital to share information publicly with a wider range of investors. The companies, either start-ups or existing, are able to raise money through a large number of people without registering a filing with the SEC.

Individuals invest through a platform or *portal* on the internet. The types of companies that may appear on a portal are regulated, and the amounts that may be raised by the company in a 12-month period are regulated, as well. Further, the amount that an individual may invest is restricted and is dependent on the individual's income and/or net worth. These investment limits also apply to a 12-month period.

In the case of a Self-Directed IRA, the net worth and/or the income of the IRA owner will determine the amount the IRA may invest. Note that the total amount invested between an owner's Self-Directed IRA and the owner's non-qualified dollars may not exceed the investment threshold allowed to an individual within the stated 12-month period.

Since these portals have start-up businesses, they may be riskier than other investments. In addition, the investments may be rather illiquid, and the Self-Directed IRA may not be able to sell the shares when needed. Some of the portals choose when to sell the investments, while other portals permit the owner of the shares to determine when to sell.

## PRECIOUS METALS

Precious metals are a popular investment for owners of Self-Directed IRAs, and the types of precious metals that may be placed in an IRA are outlined in Internal Revenue Code Section 408(m)(3). Gold, silver, platinum, and/or palladium coins or bullion that meet certain purity standards may be placed in a Self-Directed IRA.

If the standards outlined in the foregoing section of the Code are not met, the purchase is treated as a "collectible" and treated as a distribution from the Self-Directed IRA. Depending upon the type of IRA and the age of the IRA owner, this distribution may be taxable and assessed a penalty tax.

In addition to the purity standards, the law mandates that precious metals held within an IRA in the form of bullion must be stored in a nationally- or state-licensed bank or credit union, or a state-licensed trust company. These precious metals may not be stored by the IRA owner.

If the possession requirement for bullion is not met, the precious metal assets are treated as distributed from the Self-Directed IRA based upon the date the storage violation occurred. Depending on the type of Self-Directed IRA and the age of the IRA owner, this distribution may be taxable and assessed a penalty tax.

Although the Tax Court or the Department of Labor has not ruled on the storage of precious metals in the form of coins, it is the consensus of custodians and professionals that coins should be stored in a nationally- or state-licensed bank or credit union, or a state-licensed trust company.

The custodian for the Self-Directed IRA may purchase the precious metals directly from the broker identified by the

IRA owner. If the Self-Directed IRA has an IRA-LLC, the precious metals may be purchased by the IRA-LLC (if applicable) directly from the broker and they become an asset of the IRA-LLC. Although the asset may be held by the IRA-LLC, the IRA-LLC should act in accordance with IRC Section 408(m)(3) which governs the way in which precious metals should be held in an IRA.

## A WORD REGARDING UNRELATED BUSINESS INCOME TAX OR UBIT

Some of the investments described in this chapter may subject the Self-Directed IRA to Unrelated Business Income Tax or UBIT. UBIT generally applies when a Self-Directed IRA's investments receive ordinary income by providing goods or services, rather than passive income.

Passive income is generally described as interest income, dividend income, rental income, capital gain income, and/or royalty income.

Under UBIT, some of the income generated by the investments would subject the Self-Directed IRA to income tax, irrespective of the fact that the Self-Directed IRA is tax sheltered. If this were the case, it would be necessary for the Self-Directed IRA to provide the custodian a completed IRS Form 990-T Exempt Organization Business Income Tax Return to enable the custodian to pay taxes out of the Self-Directed IRA.

UBIT is something of which to be aware; it is not something to dissuade the IRA owner from the investment, if it fits within his/her retirement plan. This is yet another reason why I encourage owners of Self-Directed IRAs to consult with their team of professionals before directing the custodian to purchase investments.

## HIGHLIGHTS FROM CHAPTER 7

- An IRA-LLC may give the IRA owner checkbook access to a Self-Directed IRA's assets.
- In an IRA-LLC, if the IRA owner serves as the manager of the LLC, he/she must not be compensated.
- Money invested in a private placement may be tied up for a long time, since the issuer of the investment does not have to provide liquidity to the investors.
- The precious metals that may be held within a Self-Directed IRA are limited to gold, silver, platinum, and palladium, and must meet purity standards.
- Precious metals that do not meet purity standards are treated as a collectible and distributed; and this may have income-tax consequences to the IRA owner.
- Precious metals bullion owned by a Self-Directed IRA must be stored in a nationally-or state-licensed bank or credit union or a state-licensed trust company. Bullion may not be held in the custody of the IRA owner.
- Some investments may subject the Self-Directed IRA to Unrelated Business Income Tax (UBIT). In this case, the Self-Directed IRA would need to complete IRS Form 990-T Exempt Organization Business Income Tax Return.

## ADDITIONAL RESOURCES

**Sunwest Trust sponsors a channel on www.youtube.com called "sunwestira" in which many of the topics in this chapter are discussed. I recommend viewing the following to augment the information in this chapter.**

- "Self-Directed IRA-LLC Setup—Who Owns the LLC Membership Units?" November 11, 2015

- "IRA-LLC Custodians for a Check Book IRA Account" June 4, 2013

- "Taking Distributions From Your IRA-LLC" April 23, 2013

- "Precious Metals IRA—How Does a Precious Metals IRA Work?" September 16, 2014

- "Steps to Buying and Selling Gold Inside a Self-Directed IRA" September 25, 2015

- "IRA-LLC Precious Metal Rules, Physical Gold and Silver Possession and Storage—Be Careful" October 28, 2014

- "What Can a Self-directed IRA Invest In? Buying Private Stock in a Company I Work For" October 13, 2015

- "Invest in a Business With an IRA—It Starts With the Right IRA" May 15, 2015

- "Crowdfunding With a Self-Directed IRA" March 31, 2015

- "UBIT or Unrelated Business Income Tax" April 9, 2013

# CHAPTER 8

# SOME TYPES OF NON-TRADITIONAL ASSETS FOR A SELF-DIRECTED IRA— DEBT-BASED

Continuing with the discussion of non-traditional assets for a Self-Directed IRA, this chapter covers investments that are debt-based.

The IRA owner will want to keep in mind that the non-traditional, debt-based assets are only limited by what the custodian of the Self-Directed IRA will hold. Further, the IRA owner will want to avoid any prohibited transactions or transactions with a disqualified person or entity in acquiring the debt-based assets.

While the prohibited assets of collectibles, life insurance, and Sub-Chapter S corporations are not necessarily associated with debt-based assets, they are mentioned again for review purposes.

As I mentioned in the previous chapter, before investing, I recommend the owner of a Self-Directed IRA review any investments with his/her team of professionals.

## BUYING REAL ESTATE

Real estate is one of the most popular assets that Self-Directed IRAs hold. The real estate may be single-family homes, multi-family homes or apartments, storage units, commercial office buildings, warehouses, raw land, or even options to own or buy a piece of real estate. All documents are signed by the custodian and the title is recorded in the name of the Self-Directed IRA, for example, "Sunwest Trust Custodian for John Adams Self-Directed IRA."

When contemplating the purchase of property, the IRA owner will want to make certain there is enough cash in the Self-Directed IRA to cover the purchase price of the property and ongoing payments, as well as a reserve of cash for incidental items such as repairs, a property manager if applicable, and property taxes.

If a Self-Directed IRA does not have enough cash to buy the property outright, it may still purchase property through seller financing or a non-recourse loan. Seller financing in which the seller carries the debt through a seller-financed agreement may be arranged after a down payment.

With seller-financed real estate, the IRA owner is able to negotiate with the seller, and there is a chance the seller may be willing to accept a smaller down payment than what may otherwise be required with a non-recourse loan. In addition to maintaining close contact with the seller, the IRA owner and seller may modify the terms of the seller-financed agreement to something that is mutually acceptable to both of them. Note, the seller-financed agreement would be signed by the seller and the custodian for the Self-Directed IRA.

Seller-financed real estate allows the seller access to a larger market, since qualifying for the loan is not a criterion. The interest rate charged on the seller-financed agreement is generally higher, but still a market rate, and this may be attractive to the seller. Rather than receive the purchase price of the property in a lump sum, the seller may like the idea of the income stream on the seller-financed agreement, viewing it as an investment. Remember, with seller financing, the seller-financed agreement must be non-recourse.

If the Self-Directed IRA does not have access to seller financing, a bank non-recourse loan may be an option. As was mentioned in Chapter 6, a non-recourse loan is one in which the asset is the only item that secures the loan; the lender cannot go after the Self-Directed IRA's assets, nor can the lender go after the assets of the IRA owner.

Banks that specialize in non-recourse loans for Self-Directed IRAs may be found by doing a search on the internet. If this is the route taken, the IRA owner may expect to pay a substantial down payment equal to 30% or 40% of the mortgage.

Let's walk through an example of a Self-Directed IRA purchasing a piece of real estate. If the IRA owner is not familiar with the real estate market, the owner would be wise to engage the services of a trusted realtor. After finding the property of choice, whether it is residential, commercial, or raw land, the IRA owner will want to negotiate and agree upon a price with the seller.

After the IRA owner reviews the purchase agreement with his/her attorney, the IRA owner forwards the purchase agreement to the custodian for signature. Note, the purchaser is the Self-Directed IRA, not the IRA owner. The IRA owner will complete a Direction of Investment form directing the custodian to sign the purchase agreement and to issue a check for the amount of earnest money needed. The custodian will issue a check for that amount from the Self-Directed IRA.

Although the amount of earnest money may be modest in amount, the IRA owner should not write a personal check for this, as this could be a prohibited transaction. The paper work and check are returned to the title company.

I recommend the IRA owner go through a title company when purchasing real estate. There have been instances where the person selling the property is not the owner of the property. In addition, there could be liens, easements, or zoning violations on the property that may be undisclosed by the seller.

The closing documents should be reviewed by the IRA owner's attorney. Assuming all things are in order, all paperwork is sent to the custodian for review and signature on behalf of the Self-Directed IRA. Note, too, that the property deed is recorded in the name of the IRA, for example, "Sunwest Trust Custodian for John Adams Self-Directed IRA."

The amount due at closing will be covered by a check issued by the custodian and drawn upon the account of the Self-Directed IRA. Again, the IRA owner will be required to complete a Direction of Investment form for the amount of a down payment on a seller-financed agreement, non-recourse loan, or the full purchase price at this time.

Even though the IRA owner is actively involved in all the transactions, the IRA owner should not sign any documents or checks personally. It is the Self-Directed IRA that is purchasing the property, and it is the custodian that signs on behalf of the Self-Directed IRA. If the owner does sign any documents or issues a personal check, this could be a prohibited transaction.

Depending on the type of property, if repairs or remodeling are required on the property before it may become operational, the IRA owner will need to hire a non-disqualified person to do the work. Neither the IRA owner nor a disqualified person is allowed to complete the repairs or remodel. Any type of invoice for repairs or remodel will be directed to the custodian, for example "Sunwest Trust Custodian for John Adams Self-Directed IRA."

As mentioned earlier in this section, the IRA owner will want to maintain some cash in the Self-Directed IRA for incidentals that may arise in connection with the property, such as repairs, property taxes, ongoing payments, or a property manager.

I reference the previous chapter's section on a Self-Directed IRA-LLC. Many owners of Self-Directed IRAs set up an IRA-LLC to handle the purchase of their investments. In the foregoing example of real estate, a Self-Directed IRA with an IRA-LLC could make the purchase of real estate.

If the Self-Directed IRA has an IRA-LLC, the purchase of the real estate is facilitated by the ability of the manager to enter into contracts and write checks on behalf of the IRA-LLC. In this case when using an IRA-LLC to purchase the property, it is the IRA-LLC that owns the piece of property and holds title, not the Self-Directed IRA directly. As stated in the last chapter however, the IRA-LLC must still abide by the rules governing the IRA found in IRC Section 408(m)(3).

## PROMISSORY NOTES

A promissory note is an agreement between a lender and a borrower, in which the borrower promises to pay back a loan to the lender. In the agreement, terms are outlined regarding the amount borrowed, the term of the note, the interest rate on the note, the frequency of payment on the note, what constitutes default on the note, and the lender's remedy for default. In the context of a Self-Directed IRA, the IRA is the lender and a non-disqualified person/entity is the borrower.

Promissory Notes make an attractive investment for owners of Self-Directed IRAs. The IRA owner may either loan money to someone via a promissory note, or buy an already-existing promissory note at a discount. Many of these promissory note investments are connected to real estate. When the Self-Directed IRA deals in promissory notes, it engages in "hard-money lending or private money lending." Chances are the rate of return on these promissory notes will be higher, and the promissory notes may be less expensive than other real estate investments.

## PROMISSORY NOTES BACKED BY REAL ESTATE

When purchasing a promissory note backed by real estate, if the borrower has substantial equity in the property already, there is a good probability that the borrower will continue making payments. If the borrower defaults on a promissory note backed by real estate, the Self-Directed IRA may take back the property. This will involve legal fees and the time of the IRA owner; and the legal fees will need to be drawn from the Self-Directed IRA. Keep in mind that after the Self-Directed IRA takes the property back, it could always resell the property.

There is no market that trades in promissory notes backed by real estate, and they may be difficult to uncover. Generally, the IRA owner will want to establish a network of realtors, title companies, and escrow agents to let them know the type of promissory note the Self-Directed IRA wants to purchase.

In the case of a seller-financed agreement promissory note, the IRA owner may be able to purchase the agreement at a discount if the holder of the agreement wants to get out of the agreement or if the holder is pressed for cash.

I recommend that the IRA owner look at the property securing the note and determine if it is the type of property that the Self-Directed IRA wants to own. It is possible if the borrower defaults, that the Self-Directed IRA will own the property. If the property securing the note is not something the IRA owner would want to own in his/her Self-Directed IRA, it may be best to pass on this opportunity. Chances are there will be other opportunities.

If the Self-Directed IRA is purchasing a promissory note, the IRA owner will want to evaluate whether the promissory note is a wise investment. A promissory note secured by property may be an attractive investment and is more attractive than an unsecured promissory note. Also, the IRA owner will want to get a copy of the promissory note agreement between borrower and lender, determine if the note actually amortizes, and get the payment history on the note.

By requesting a title search, the IRA owner will be able to determine whether the person or entity selling the promissory note is actually the owner of the promissory note. In addition, the IRA owner will be able to determine the promissory note's position.

The title search will ascertain if there is a mortgage, tax lien, or Home Owners' Association Dues (HOA) due on the property and may identify other issues. For example, in the state of New Mexico, the water bills stay with the property; the bills are not attached to the property owner.

Also, if the property previously had a gas station on it, there could be environmental issues attached to the property. These issues could affect the IRA owner's decision to buy the note for the Self-Directed IRA, and would impact the rate of return. Again, I recommend the IRA owner consult with his/her team of professionals before making an investment decision.

## A PROMISSORY NOTE SUCCESS STORY

Opportunities for promissory notes exist everywhere, and I want to share the success story of three of our clients who are sisters.

One of these sisters has a son who buys houses, fixes them up, and then flips them for a nice profit. In order to generate the cash flow needed for this, the son borrowed money using short-term loans through a hard-money lender; the rate he paid for these loans was a rather high market rate. Our client wanted to help her son, but knew she was unable to loan her son money for this business from her Self-Directed IRA. Her son was a disqualified person, and this would have been a prohibited transaction.

Our client learned that her two sisters who owned traditional-asset IRAs were unhappy with the volatility in the stock market. The two sisters indicated that they would be happy to loan their nephew money from their IRA, because they knew of his work and trusted him. The sister who owned the Self-Directed IRA convinced her two sisters to directly transfer their traditional-asset IRAs to Self-Directed IRAs with our company.

The two sisters began loaning money to their nephew for the purpose of flipping houses. This resulted in their receiving better returns on their investment, and avoiding the volatility of the stock market. Since they trusted their nephew and their sister, they knew the loans would be repaid; plus they could help out a family member. Note that for Internal Revenue Code purposes, according to Section 4975 (e)(2), the nephew was not considered a family member, and was not a disqualified person.

The nephew received the loans at a lower market rate than he was receiving from the hard-money lender; and as a result, the nephew repaid the loans more quickly. In addition, the nephew expanded his business and employed more people locally. Everyone in this transaction benefitted.

## TRUST DEEDS AND MORTGAGES

Private money has become an alternative source of funds for individuals looking to invest in real estate. This has become an attractive investment for Self-Directed IRAs, since the banks, mortgage bankers, and mortgage companies have tightened up their loan requirements.

In addition to the promissory note agreement that outlines the amount borrowed, the term of the note, the interest rate on the note, the frequency of payment on the note, what constitutes default on the note, and the lender's remedy for default; the Self-Directed IRA will need either a mortgage or trust deed. This is because the promissory note is usually not recorded at the county's land office.

It is a mortgage or trust deed that identifies the real estate as collateral or security for the loan, and the mortgage or trust deed is used to record the property outlined in the promissory note at the county's land office. The mortgage or trust deed secure the promissory note.

Mortgages and trust deeds generally contain a clause called an acceleration clause that allows the lender to demand the entire balance of the loan if the borrower defaults on the loan. If the borrower doesn't pay, the property can be foreclosed and sold. The lender is required to notify the borrower before activation of the acceleration clause. If the borrower doesn't pay, the lender may begin foreclosure proceedings. The foreclosure cost must be paid by the Self-Directed IRA, and that is a good reason to keep some liquid cash in the Self-Directed IRA.

## MORTGAGES

In a mortgage, there are two parties to the contract, the lender which is the Self-Directed IRA, and the borrower which is a non-disqualified person. The Self-Directed IRA holds the mortgage while the borrower makes payments. In this case, the Self-Directed IRA would generally want an escrow agent or third-party processor to keep track of the payments and forward them to the Self-Directed IRA.

If the borrower defaults on the loan, the subsequent foreclosure takes place through the court system. Once the loan is satisfied by foreclosure, the Self-Directed IRA is free to sell the property and reinvest the cash from the sale. The attorney on the IRA owner's team of professionals can walk the IRA owner through this whole process.

## TRUST DEEDS

If a trust deed is used, there are three parties: the borrower which is called the trustor, the beneficiary which is the lender or the Self-Directed IRA, and the trustee which is a third party, such as an attorney or title company. Over the repayment period, the trustee holds the title to the property. The Self-Directed IRA would generally want an escrow agent or third-party processor to keep track of the payments and forward them to the Self-Directed IRA.

If the borrower (trustor) defaults on the loan, the subsequent foreclosure does not take place through the court system. For example, in New Mexico, if the borrower (trustor) defaults on a promissory note secured by a trust-deed contract there are rules the trust-deed contract holder must follow to execute a foreclosure and termination of the trust-deed contract. Every state is different, however; and the IRA owner should consult the attorney on his/her team of professionals.

If the loan is satisfied by foreclosure, the proceeds are transferred to the Self-Directed IRA (beneficiary/lender), and the trustee conveys title of the property to the buyer, the buyer's lender, or a new trustee. If the loan is satisfied in full through regularly-scheduled payments, the trustee conveys title of the property to the borrower.

## SUMMARY

I recommend the owner of a Self-Directed IRA consult with his/her team of professionals before engaging in any promissory note, trust deed investment, and/or mortgage. Promissory notes, mortgages, and trust deeds require properly-worded documents to protect the lender, in this case, the Self-Directed IRA.

Further, not all states permit mortgages and/or trust deeds. Some permit both, but others limit the document to either a mortgage or a trust deed. In addition, while the interest rate charged in the promissory note must be commercially viable, some states impose prohibitions on the rate that may be charged. This is where the services of the IRA owner's team of professionals may be invaluable.

## NOTES SECURED BY EQUIPMENT AND UNSECURED NOTES

The foregoing paragraphs discussed promissory notes secured by real estate. It is possible to secure a promissory note with equipment, fixtures, or other property. The Self-Directed IRA would obtain a promissory note outlining the details and terms of the loan, and a security agreement in which the equipment being used as collateral would be described.

In this instance, the Self-Directed IRA would file a legal document called a National Financing Statement, also known as a Uniform Commercial Code-1 (UCC-1), with the secretary of state in the state in which the collateral is located. This filing shows that the Self-Directed IRA is a creditor and identifies the equipment that has been used as collateral for the loan. With this document in place, the borrower is unable to pledge the same equipment as security for a loan. Upon repayment of the note, the Self-Directed IRA would file a release and the property backing the loan would be free and clear.

Promissory notes may be unsecured, and this is a riskier type of investment than a secured promissory note. Unsecured promissory notes generally have lower loan amounts and higher interest rates, due to the fact that there is nothing securing the debt to the lender. These notes also have shorter terms. The lender, in this case the Self-Directed IRA, is relying only on the promise of the borrower to pay. Before engaging in an unsecured promissory note, I recommend the owner of the Self-Directed IRA examine the borrower's credit history.

Be aware that many Ponzi schemes use unsecured promissory notes. I strongly suggest that the IRA owner consult with his/her team of professionals before investing. Do not simply trust the person to whom the loan is being made.

## PROPERTY TAX LIENS

Property tax liens may be another attractive investment for owners of Self-Directed IRAs. When an owner of a property fails to pay property taxes to the municipality in which the property is located, the municipality issues a tax lien on the property. This is a legal claim on the taxes which are owed. Consequently, the property owner is unable to sell or refinance the property until the taxes are paid and the lien is removed.

After issuing a tax lien, many municipalities issue a tax lien certificate for the amount of taxes due, plus interest, and any penalties. The municipality then auctions these tax lien certificates to investors, and the highest bid wins. Once the tax lien certificate is acquired, the municipality requires the new lien holder to pay off the tax lien immediately which includes taxes, interest, and penalties. Also, the new lien holder is required to notify the property owner in writing that the lien has been acquired and consequently, there is a new lien holder.

The new lien holder advises the property owner to pay off the lien, including interest and penalties; the time over which the lien is paid off generally runs from six months to three years. At the end of this term, if the property owner has not paid the lien off, the new owner of the lien has the authority to foreclose on the property. Note, the liens may have expiration dates after the redemption period (the time the property owner is given to repay the lien), as well. After the expiration date, the lien becomes worthless.

Tax liens are regulated by the state and county, and the rates of interest charged on the lien are regulated by the state. The county treasurer has information regarding where to obtain a list of the properties for auction and when the auctions are scheduled. Note that property tax liens are not offered in every state, nor is an investor in property tax liens limited to the acquisition of liens only in his/her state of residence.

If a Self-Directed IRA wants to invest in property tax liens, I recommend the IRA owner be knowledgeable in real estate or consult with a trusted realtor. Before acquiring a tax lien, the IRA owner should decide the type of property on which to pursue the tax lien. Tax liens are issued on residential property, commercial property, and raw or developed land.

The IRA owner should also seek to acquire knowledge about the property on which a bid for the lien will be placed. If the property is in disrepair, it may mean that the property owner is unable or unwilling to pay the property taxes. In addition to the condition of the property, there may be environmental issues attached to the property.

I recommend that the IRA owner look at the property securing the lien to determine if that is the type of property the Self-Directed IRA wants to own. It is possible if the property owner defaults, that the Self-Directed IRA will own the property. If the property on which the lien is filed is not something the Self-Directed IRA would want to own, it may be best to pass on this opportunity. Chances are there will be other opportunities.

## A WORD REGARDING UNRELATED BUSINESS INCOME TAX OR UBIT

As I mentioned in the previous chapter, some of the investments described in this chapter may subject the Self-

Directed IRA to Unrelated Business Income Tax or UBIT. UBIT generally applies when an IRA's investments receive ordinary income by providing goods or services, rather than passive income.

Passive income is generally described as interest income, dividend income, rental income, capital gain income, and/or royalty income. The UBIT may apply when the Self-Directed IRA engages in a non-recourse loan, as well.

Under UBIT, some of the income generated by the investments would subject the Self-Directed IRA to income tax, irrespective of the fact that the Self-Directed IRA is tax sheltered. It would be necessary for the Self-Directed IRA to provide the custodian a completed IRS Form 990-T Exempt Organization Business Income Tax Return to enable the custodian to pay taxes out of the Self-Directed IRA.

UBIT is something of which to be aware; it is not something to dissuade the owner from the investment if it fits within one's retirement plan. This is yet another reason why I encourage owners of Self-Directed IRAs to consult with their team of professionals before directing the custodian to purchase investments.

In the last chapter of this book, I discuss Sunwest Trust and the custodial services it has to offer owners of Self-Directed IRAs.

## HIGHLIGHTS FROM CHAPTER 8

- **IRA owners with real estate in their Self-Directed IRAs will want to make certain there is enough cash in their Self-Directed IRA to cover incidental items such as repairs; a property manager, if applicable; and property taxes.**
- **Seller financing may be an option for the IRA owner who does not have enough cash in his/her Self-Directed IRA to purchase the property outright.**
- **While trust deeds or mortgages are attractive investments for a Self-Directed IRA, not all states permit them.**
- **Promissory notes may be secured by property other than real estate, such as equipment.**
- **The IRA owner should make certain that the property which secures a property tax lien is something that the Self-Directed IRA would want to own, because the Self-Directed IRA may ultimately end up with the property.**
- **Some IRA investments may subject the Self-Directed IRA to Unrelated Business Income Tax (UBIT). In this case, the Self-Directed IRA would need to complete IRS Form 990-T Exempt Organization Business Income Tax Return.**

## ADDITIONAL RESOURCES

Sunwest Trust sponsors a channel on www.youtube.com called "sunwestira" in which many of the topics in this chapter are discussed. I recommend viewing the following to augment the information in this chapter.

- "Buying Real Estate in an IRA—Does It Work?" August 6, 2015

- "What Investments Can Be Held in an IRA—Real Estate IRA Investment" August 12, 2014

- "Keep Your Self-Directed IRA from 'Breaking Bad'" October 15, 2013

- "Self-Directed IRA Condo Investing—Investment Finders Series"
  Part 1 September 17, 2013
  Part 2 September 24, 2013
  Part 3 October 22, 2013
  Final Part December 4, 2013

- "Investing in Real estate Notes-Part 1 What Are Notes?" February 25, 2014

- "Investing in Real estate Notes-Part 2 Where to Find Notes for Sale" March 4, 2014

- "Investing in Real estate Notes-Part 3 Pros and Cons" March 11, 2014

- "Investing in Real estate Notes-Part 4 Evaluating Notes and Due Diligence" March 18, 2014

- "Investing in Real estate Notes-Part 5 Avoiding Pitfalls" March 25, 2014

- "Investing in Real estate Notes-Part 6 Brokering Notes Without Using Your Own Money" April 1, 2014

- "Investing in Real estate Notes-Part 7 Buying in an IRA, UBIT Ramifications" April 8, 2014

- "Investing in Real estate Notes-Part 8 The Process of Buying" April 15, 2014

- "Closing Through a Title Company and Other Investment Advice" April 30, 2013

- "UBIT or Unrelated Business Income Tax" April 9, 2013

- "Leveraged IRA–Non-Recourse Debt in IRA–Borrow Money, Buy Real Estate in IRA–UDFI–Filing IRS Form 990-T" December 10, 2015

IRA Wealth: Revolutionary IRA Strategies for Real Estate Investment
by Patrick W. Rice

Invest in Debt
By Jim Napier

# CHAPTER 9

# SUNWEST TRUST, INC., CUSTODIAN OF CHOICE

"Choose the right tool for the job you are wanting to do. We at Sunwest Trust are the right tool when you need us."

Terry White
President & CEO Sunwest Trust, Inc.

I hope this book has been helpful. I wrote this book as an informational guide for those who may be interested in Self-Directed IRAs. As a former financial services representative, I recognize the importance of retirement planning. It is important for individuals to learn the many options of which they can avail themselves.

It was my intention to give a broad overview of what owners of Self-Directed IRAs may expect and some of the investments they may purchase. As I mentioned previously, Self-Directed IRAs are not for everyone. But, for anyone wishing to set up a Self-Directed IRA, I invite you to look at Sunwest Trust for your Self-Directed IRA needs and make it your custodian of choice.

## HISTORY

Sunwest Trust, Inc. is a privately-owned company that has been in operation for over 28 years; it is located in Albuquerque, New Mexico. The company began as a small escrow company in October 1987 with one employee; it was called First Financial Escrow, Inc. In the first 10 years of business, First Financial Escrow grew by accepting new accounts and by acquiring small escrow companies in the region. It established a reputation for being honest, hardworking, and fair.

In 1997, First Financial Escrow purchased all of the escrow accounts from Sunwest Bank and at that time, changed its name to Sunwest Escrow, LC. Through this purchase, the number of escrow accounts under management increased from 2,000 to 10,000.

As one of the shareholders at the time and based upon my financial services background, I wanted to expand the business into Self-Directed Individual Retirement Accounts, as well. In 2003, Sunwest Trust was formed, and shortly thereafter the company was granted its trust powers from the State of New Mexico Financial Institutions Division. This made Sunwest Trust the only company in New Mexico with the ability to act as an escrow agent and as a custodian for Individual Retirement Accounts.

In 2004 as Sunwest Trust, we set up 100 Self-Directed Individual Retirement Accounts; and I had the responsibility for establishing these accounts. In 2005, we added another 100 Self-Directed Individual Retirement Accounts, and I trained another employee in account set up. Like me, she has been affiliated with the company for 28 years; she is the Executive Vice President.

Sunwest Trust, through our employees' hard work and dedicated service, has continued to grow. Currently, we have 25 employees and we service the Self-Directed Individual Retirement Accounts for three other companies, as well as our own. We service over 9,000 IRA accounts and have close to $1.1 billion dollars of assets under custody. Sunwest Trust is accredited by the Better Business Bureau and is a member of the Retirement Industry Trust Association.

Since the first day of operations, we have been regulated by the State of New Mexico. Routinely, Sunwest Trust undergoes audits by the state. Audits of our trust accounts are made annually, and there is an IRS-type audit conducted annually by an independent agency.

**PHILOSOPHY**

Sunwest Trust has earned a reputation of being honest, hardworking, and fair. Training and education are important components of these standards, not only for the Sunwest Trust employees, but for the company's clients, as well. We listened to our clients and learned how to become the type of company with whom they want to do business.

I believe that clients will be happier with their Sunwest Trust experience when they have all the information at their disposal. At Sunwest Trust we have worked to accomplish this. Our website contains information and forms for both our Escrow Division and our Self-Directed IRA Division. Fee schedules for each division are easily accessible from this website, as well as access to clients' respective accounts.

We accept Self-Directed IRAs from all over the United States; our operations are not confined just to New Mexico. Further, we provide telephone hours from 7:00 AM until 5:00 PM Mountain Time to accommodate those clients on the east coast.

This book has stressed the fact that custodians do not provide legal, tax, or accounting advice; and Sunwest Trust follows this procedure. We have, however, made a resource for general questions available on our website. The "Ask the Experts" tab on the site addresses general questions regarding provisions of the Internal Revenue Code (IRC), and rulings by the Department of Labor (DOL), and how they relate to Self-Directed IRAs. We have contracted with an independent consulting firm to provide this service.

For the last five years, we have electronically published a monthly newsletter with topics covering information for Self-Directed IRA holders that pertain to different types of investments to prohibited-transaction issues. For the last six years, we have produced and posted videos to our Sunwest Trust IRA Channel on YouTube. These videos, which are generally four to six minutes in length, address different types of Self-Directed IRA investments, how to purchase the investments correctly, give examples of prohibited transactions, inform about how to fill out some Self-Directed IRA forms, and answer questions posed by actual clients.

Our Sunwest Trust employees are trained so that whomever answers the phone in the Escrow Division or the Self-Directed IRA Division is able to respond to your question without having to transfer you to another person. Employees are empowered and encouraged to make decisions. As the CEO, I support this philosophy; and employees know that I will support them as long as they can demonstrate that the decision at which they arrived was based upon our four core values: integrity, compassion, reliability, and ownership.

Training does not stop once the employees have mastered their positions; there is ongoing training in successful business principles and life principles so that employees may become more well-rounded.

In regard to employees' health and well-being, Sunwest Trust has a gym on site. Employees may go to the gym on their lunch hour to work out, or they may take advantage of the trainers that are on site five times per week. The trainers conduct classes at the end of the work day, and there are different levels of workouts offered so that all may benefit.

Sunwest Trust is also an active partner in national and community affairs. Our company donates a percentage of its profits each year to various charities; some are local charities and others are part of national organizations. The focus of these charities is homelessness for adults and children, domestic violence, and veterans' health and well-being. Employees are encouraged to take an active part in volunteering for these charities. Often, Sunwest Trust volunteers as a group and donates their time on site at a local charity.

## SERVICES

As has been noted in previous chapters, not all custodians provide for the different types of non-traditional investments outlined in this book. I am pleased to say that Sunwest Trust acts as a custodian for all the investments outlined in this book.

Sunwest Trust permits IRA-LLCs and also permits IRA owners to act as non-compensated managers of their Self-Directed IRA-LLCs. We also serve as custodian for precious metals held within a Self-Directed IRA and insure the metals are stored in an approved facility according to the Internal Revenue Code.

Although applications for Self-Directed IRAs may be

completed on line, Sunwest Trust requires that the application contain the original signature. This necessitates the application being mailed to Sunwest Trust. Online applications are available regardless of the type of IRA that is being registered. This includes the Traditional IRA, Roth IRA, SEP-IRA, and IRA-SIMPLE. There are also forms available online to request a custodian-to-custodian direct transfer to a Self-Directed IRA.

Note that since every custodian requires an acceptable form of government-issued identification, such as a driver's license or a passport, this may require mailing a clear copy of the identification, if an applicant is unable to scan and electronically transfer (upload) the identification.

Sunwest Trust charges a flat fee for its Self-Directed IRA services, regardless of the number of assets or the value of those assets; the fee is not based upon the dollar amount of assets under management, nor is an IRA owner charged for each type of asset he/she has in the account. The fee for a Self-Directed IRA with precious metals is slightly higher than the fee for a Self-Directed IRA without precious metals, due to the storage requirement.

In addition, there is an application fee and charges for outgoing services such as checks, wire transfers, or overnight mail. A fee is charged when the account is closed or transferred; a deposit is recharacterized; and/or an account is converted. There is also a fee for any special handling. Other than the fees I've just listed, there are no additional fees, hidden or otherwise. All fees are displayed on our website.

Sunwest Trust requires that a minimum of $300.00 in cash be kept in the Self-Directed IRA. Any cash in a Self-Directed IRA is deposited into a bank where it earns a prevailing rate of interest and it is also FDIC-insured up to $250,000.00. If there is more than $250,000.00 cash in a Self-Directed IRA, the funds are split up between several banks so that the full amount of FDIC-insurance protection is available. Sunwest Trust has established relationships with several banks in Albuquerque to accomplish this: US Bank, Peoples Bank, Washington Federal, Bank of the West, and Bank of New Mexico.

## INNOVATIONS

Earlier in this chapter, I indicated that we learned from our clients and listened to them. I am pleased to say that we created and designed two tools for our Self-Directed IRA owners: *The Self-Directed Beneficiaries' Information Form* described in Chapter 4; and a free website called *myirallcbookkeeper.com* to be used by IRA owners who have IRA-LLCs as described in Chapter 7.

*The Self-Directed Beneficiaries' Information Form*

This form requests the beneficiary's(ies') name(s) and information, the types of investments held in the account, and other relevant information such as IRA distribution rules for beneficiaries, and the contacts and/or brokers for the investments held in the IRA. In addition, if the Self-Directed IRA owns an IRA-LLC, this form shows the bank and account number for the IRA-LLC. The IRA owner authorizes Sunwest Trust to hold this information, and it is kept secure until your beneficiaries need it. At that time, the information is released to your beneficiary(ies).

As part of this service, we encourage our Self-Directed IRA owners to update this form every year, especially if changes have been made to the investments. This form was designed and created with our Self-Directed IRA owners in mind, so that their loved ones would have an easier time when an unplanned disaster happens. They may never need this information, but it is always a great idea to be prepared.

*Myirallcbookkeeper.com*

This is an interactive website designed for IRA owners that hold an IRA-LLC in their Self-Directed IRAs. It is important to keep adequate and precise records of the IRA-LLC's accounts, expenditures, and investments; and that is what this program does. Sunwest Trust provides this service free of charge for its Self-Directed IRA clients.

After registering on the *myirallcbookkeeper.com* website, the IRA owner completes information regarding the IRA-LLC's checking account. As may be recalled from Chapter 7, the IRA-LLC is a way to give check book access to the IRA owner. The IRA-LLC's bank information is recorded on this site, and checks are printed for the IRA owner's use.

Each time the IRA owner completes the request for a check with the amount and the name of the party involved, the program questions whether or not this investment is a prohibited transaction. This is a safeguard for the IRA owner and a reminder that the IRA owner might want to review the investment with one's team of professionals, if that has not been done already.

As another safeguard, *myirallcbookkeeper.com* will not allow the IRA owner the ability to print a check made out to himself or herself. As may be recalled from Chapter 7, the IRA owner may not make a distribution from the IRA-LLC to himself or herself; any distributions must come from the custodian of the Self-Directed IRA.

The interactive nature of this program allows the IRA owner to keep track of investments and also update the value of those investments, if warranted. At the end of the year, *myirallcbookkeeper.com* prints a report of all transactions and assets owned by the IRA-LLC. This report may be given to the IRA owner's accountant and can be used in establishing the values of the IRA-LLC for IRS Form 5498. IRS Form 5498 is created by the Self-Directed IRA custodian, based upon the values provided by the IRA owner.

## SUMMARY

I am proud of our company and our employees, and what we have accomplished. We have a dedicated group of people who enjoy what they do, and want to make the Self-Directed IRA experience a pleasure for all of our clients.

If you are considering investing in a Self-Directed IRA or have a Self-Directed IRA at another custodian and do not feel you are getting the service that you want or deserve, please consider Sunwest Trust as your Custodian of Choice.

**SUNWEST TRUST, INC.**
**10600 MENAUL BLVD. NE**
**ALBUQUERQUE, NEW MEXICO 87112**
**PHONE: 505.237.2225**
**FAX: 505.275.1554**
**TOLL-FREE: 1.800.642.7167**
**WEBSITE: www.sunwesttrust.com**
**EMAIL: tlw@sunwesttrust.com**

63362083R00076

Made in the USA
Charleston, SC
02 November 2016